Eyewitness
VOLCANO

Vesuv. Ash rain of the eruption
(March 1944: days 22, 23, 24, 25, 26)

Skull from Herculaneum

Lava bomb

Sulfur

Gray-Milne seismograph, 1885

Carbonized bread from Pompeii

Cut peridot

Gem-quality olivine

Cut and uncut diamond

Carbonized walnuts from Pompeii

Preserved eggs from Pompeii

Body cast from Pompeii

Pele's hair

Voyager 1
space probe

Eyewitness
VOLCANO

Written by
SUSANNA VAN ROSE

Bottle melted in
eruption of
Mount Pelée

Perfume bottle
melted in eruption
of Mount Pelée

Zhang Heng's
earthquake detector

DK Publishing

Title page from
Campi Phlegraei

Fork and pocket
watch damaged
in eruption of
Mount Pelée

Seneca, Roman philosopher who
wrote about earthquake of 62 CE

DK

LONDON, NEW YORK,
MELBOURNE, MUNICH, and DELHI

Project editor Scott Steedman
Art editor Christian Sévigny
Designer Yaël Freudmann
Managing editor Helen Parker
Managing art editor Julia Harris
Production Louise Barratt
Picture research Kathy Lockley
Special photography James Stevenson
Editorial consultants Professor John Guest and Dr. Robin Adams

THIS EDITION
Consultant Douglas Palmer
Editors Francesca Baines, Sue Nicholson,
Victoria Heywood-Dunne, Marianne Petrou
Art editors Catherine Goldsmith, David Ball
Managing editors Andrew Macintyre, Camilla Hallinan
Managing art editors Jane Thomas, Martin Wilson
Publishing manager Sunita Gahir
Production editors Siu Yin Ho, Andy Hilliard
Production controllers Jenny Jacoby, Pip Tinsley
Picture research Sarah Pownall, Jenny Baskaya
DK picture library Rose Horridge, Emma Shepherd
U.S. editorial Beth Hester, Beth Sutinis
U.S. design & DTP Dirk Kaufman, Milos Orlovic
U.S. production Chris Avgherinos

Mining
transit

This Eyewitness ® Guide has been conceived by
Dorling Kindersley Limited and Editions Gallimard

This edition first published in the United States in 2008
by DK Publishing, Inc., 375 Hudson Street, New York, New York 10014

Copyright © 1992, © 2002, © 2004, © 2008 Dorling Kindersley Limited
08 09 10 11 12 10 9 8 7 6 5 4 3 2 1
ED631 – 04/08

A catalog record for this book is available from the Library of Congress.
ISBN 978-0-7566-3780-4

Color reproduction by Colourscan, Singapore
Printed and bound by Leo Paper Products Ltd., China

Discover more at
www.dk.com

Lava stalagmite

Figure of Zhang Heng,
Chinese seismologist

Contents

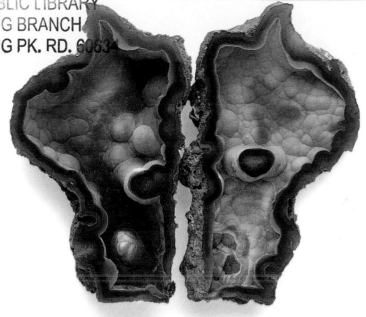

Brown agate

An unstable Earth

VOLCANOES AND EARTHQUAKES are nature run wild. A volcano in eruption may bleed rivers of red-hot lava or spew great clouds of ash and gas into the atmosphere. During a severe earthquake, the solid ground can shake so violently that entire cities are reduced to rubble. These events are disasters that can kill thousands of people. But most volcanoes and earthquakes cause little damage to people or property. They are natural events that happen all over the globe (though in some places more than others). The most familiar volcanoes are graceful, cone-shaped mountains. But any hole through which lava reaches Earth's surface is a volcano. Some are broad and flat, and most are found deep beneath the sea.

THE PERFECT VOLCANO
The graceful slopes of Mount Fujiyama in Japan rise 12,388 ft (3,776 m) above sea level. This dormant (sleeping) volcano (pp.38–39) is an almost perfect cone. Some Japanese believe that gods live at the summit, which is always shrouded in snow, and often in cloud as well. This view of the peak is one of a set of 36 prints by Katsushika Hokusai (1760–1849).

WALL PAINTING
Nearly 8,000 years old, this wall painting of an eruption of Hassan Dag in Turkey is the earliest known picture of a volcano. The houses of a town, Çatal Hüyük, can be seen at the mountain's foot.

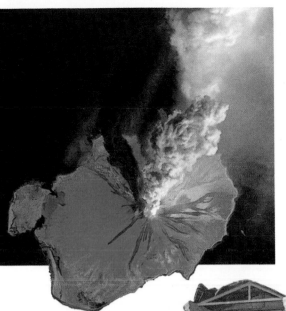

ASH TREATMENT
Eruptions may destroy homes and kill people, but they have their useful side. In Japan, being buried in warm volcanic ash is thought to cure various ailments.

ASHY VOLCANO
Ashy volcanic eruptions (pp.14–15) are unpredictable, and observing them from the ground is dangerous. This false-color photo of Augustine Volcano in Alaska was taken from the safety of a satellite. The ash cloud is being blasted 7 miles (11 km) high, through the atmosphere, from where it will be carried far and wide before falling back to Earth.

OLD FAITHFUL
Geysers are springs that spit superheated water and steam high into the air (pp.36–37). They are caused by volcanic heat acting on trapped ground-water. This American geyser, Old Faithful, has erupted every hour for at least 100 years.

BACK FROM THE DEAD
Most of the people killed or injured in earthquakes are crushed when buildings collapse. This fresco by the 14th-century painter Giotto shows a boy killed in a quake in Assisi, Italy. Legend has it that St. Francis of Assisi brought the boy back to life.

SPITTING FIRE
Mount Etna rises 11,122 ft (3,390 m) over the Italian island of Sicily, and is one of the highest mountains and most active volcanoes in Europe. Fountains of gassy lava often spew from the summit (left). Lava flows from a sizable eruption in 2001 destroyed ski-lift pylons, but stopped short of the village of Nicolisi. The nearby town of Catania is occasionally showered with ash from explosions.

SAN FRANCISCO, 1989
In 1906, San Francisco was flattened by an enormous earthquake. The shaking left large parts of the city in ruins, and the fires that followed added to the destruction. Earthquakes of this size seem to rock the area every hundred years or so. A smaller quake on October 17, 1989 shook many houses near the waterfront right off their foundations. Some 62 people died in the 15 seconds of shaking.

Fire from below

A **JOURNEY TO THE CENTER OF EARTH** would produce quite a sweat. Some 120 miles (200 km) down, the temperature is 2,730°F (1,500°C) and the rocks are white-hot. Many metals melt long before they get this hot. But because of the intense pressure inside Earth, the rocks, though soft, are not molten (liquid) until much deeper. Most of the molten rock erupted by volcanoes comes from the top of the mantle, 60 to 180 miles (100 to 300 km) down. Here, pockets of magma (molten rock) are produced when the right conditions allow a little melting in between the crystals of the rock. Because magma is hotter and lighter than the surrounding rocks, it rises, melting some of the rocks it passes on the way. If it manages to find a way to the surface, the magma will erupt as lava.

HOT AS HELL
The Irish artist James Barry painted this view of Hell in 1788. In the Christian religion, Hell is described as a fiery underworld where sinners burn in eternal damnation.

CHANNELS OF FIRE
The center of Earth is hard to imagine. In this 17th-century engraving, Athanasius Kircher envisioned a fiery core that fed all the volcanoes on the surface. We now know that because of the high pressures, little of the planet's interior is liquid, and there are no subterranean connections between volcanoes.

Red-hot lava (liquid rock) shoots out of a volcano in a curtain of fire

BASALT
The ocean floors that cover three-quarters of Earth's surface are made of a dark, heavy volcanic rock called basalt.

THIN-SKINNED
If Earth were the size of an apple, the tectonic plates (pp.10–13) that cover it would be no thicker than the apple's skin. Like the fruit, the planet has a core. This is surrounded by the mantle—the flesh of the apple.

INTO THE CRATER
Jules Verne's famous story *Journey to the Center of the Earth* begins with a perilous descent into the crater of Mount Etna. After many underground adventures, the heroes resurface in a volcanic eruption in Iceland.

GRANITE
The continents are made of a variety of rocks that are mostly lighter in weight and color than basalt. On average, their composition is similar to granite.

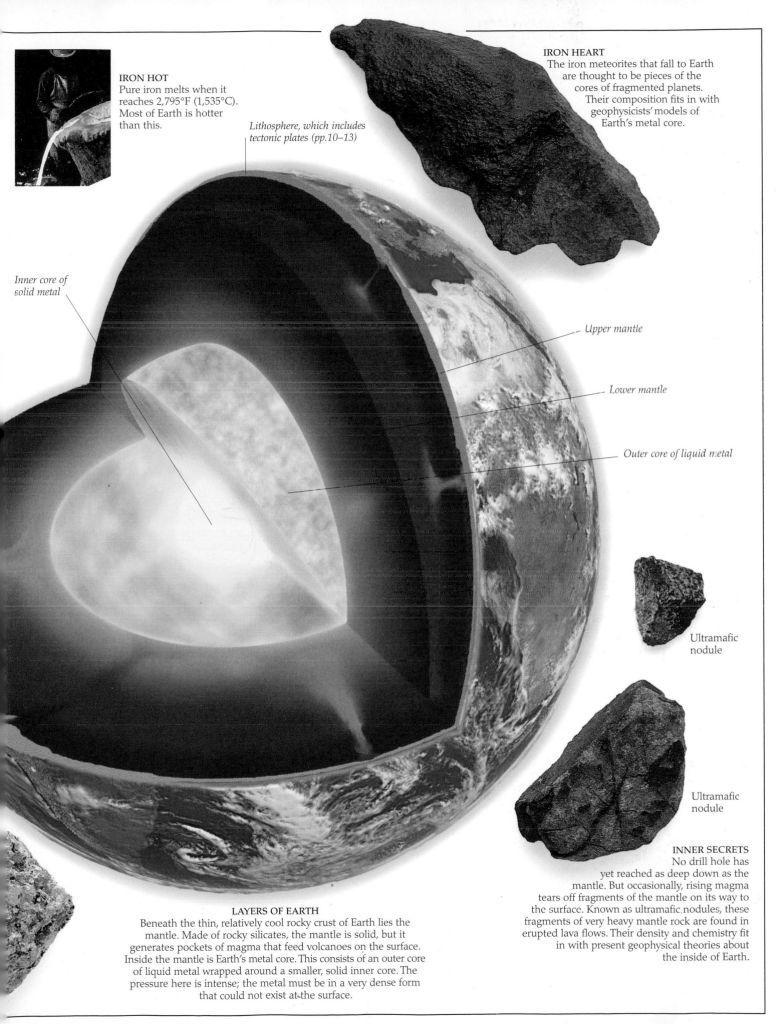

IRON HOT
Pure iron melts when it reaches 2,795°F (1,535°C). Most of Earth is hotter than this.

Lithosphere, which includes tectonic plates (pp.10–13)

IRON HEART
The iron meteorites that fall to Earth are thought to be pieces of the cores of fragmented planets. Their composition fits in with geophysicists' models of Earth's metal core.

Inner core of solid metal

Upper mantle

Lower mantle

Outer core of liquid metal

Ultramafic nodule

Ultramafic nodule

INNER SECRETS
No drill hole has yet reached as deep down as the mantle. But occasionally, rising magma tears off fragments of the mantle on its way to the surface. Known as ultramafic nodules, these fragments of very heavy mantle rock are found in erupted lava flows. Their density and chemistry fit in with present geophysical theories about the inside of Earth.

LAYERS OF EARTH
Beneath the thin, relatively cool rocky crust of Earth lies the mantle. Made of rocky silicates, the mantle is solid, but it generates pockets of magma that feed volcanoes on the surface. Inside the mantle is Earth's metal core. This consists of an outer core of liquid metal wrapped around a smaller, solid inner core. The pressure here is intense; the metal must be in a very dense form that could not exist at the surface.

CARRYING THE WEIGHT OF THE WORLD
The ancient Romans believed that the god Atlas held the sky on his shoulders. In this statue from the first century CE, he is carrying the entire globe.

The world on a plate

VOLCANOES AND EARTHQUAKES are more common in some parts of the world than others. This was known early in the 19th century, but it was not until the 1960s, when the secrets of the deep ocean floor began to be revealed, that scientists found an explanation. This became known as the theory of plate tectonics ("tectonic" comes from a Greek word that means "building"). The tectonic theory says that Earth's surface is fragmented into pieces that fit together like odd-shaped paving stones. Called tectonic plates, these chunks of Earth's skin move across its surface in response to forces and movements deep within the planet. The plate boundaries, where plates collide, rub together, or move apart, are areas of intense geological activity. Most volcanoes and earthquakes occur at these boundaries, and the nature of the boundary dictates the nature of the volcanoes and earthquakes that occur there.

CONTINENTAL DRIFTER
German meteorologist Alfred Wegener (1880–1930) coined the term "continental drift." He saw the fit of the coastlines of South America and Africa, and their similarities in terms of geology and fossils, and suggested that they had once been attached. However, at the time there was no known way that the continents could have moved apart. For more than half a century his ideas were largely ignored by geophysicists. Only when spreading ridges (pp.24–25) were discovered 40 years later was his theory accepted.

RING OF FIRE
More than 1,500 active volcanoes on Earth rise above sea level, and every year there are over a million earthquakes, mostly tiny tremors too small to be felt. In this map, the black cones are volcanoes and the red zones are prone to earthquakes. Both are common along the "Ring of Fire," the edges of the plates that form the floor of the Pacific Ocean.

LESSONS OF HISTORY

This plaster cast shows a man killed in the eruption of Mount Vesuvius that devastated the Roman towns of Pompeii and Herculaneum in 79 CE (pp.26–31). Contemporary accounts and the more recent excavations still tell the horrific story of the eruption.

LIVING ON THE RING OF FIRE

There are more than 70 active volcanoes in Japan, and few weeks go by without an earthquake or two. This huge quake in 1925 damaged the historic city of Kyoto.

Iceland sits on top of the spreading Mid-Atlantic Ridge (pp.24–25)

Like Japan, Kamchatka is part of the Pacific "Ring of Fire"

Alaska and the Aleutian Islands have many volcanoes and earthquakes

The Mid-Atlantic Ridge is part of the largest mountain range in the world

The island of Réunion was formed by a hot spot (pp.22–23) that was under India 30 million years ago

Antarctica is surrounded by new ocean made by spreading ridges (pp.24–25)

Indonesia, home to over 125 active volcanoes, is at the boundary of two plates

There are no active volcanoes in Australia, which sits in the middle of a plate

DRIFTING PLATES

This globe has been colored to highlight the tectonic plates. One plate may contain both continent and ocean crust. The Australian Plate, for instance, includes a large part of the Indian Ocean. It is thus the plates, and not the continents, that are on the move.

Mount Erebus, an active volcano in Antarctica

11

Continued on next page

FIRELAND
Iceland might better be called Fireland, as it is a land of volcanoes and geysers. The island is made almost entirely of volcanic rocks like those found on the deep ocean floor. It has gradually built up above sea level through intense and prolonged eruptions.

Moving plates

Wherever tectonic plates meet, the great stresses of the jostling rocks are released in earthquakes. Most volcanoes also occur at plate boundaries, where melting rock forms magma that erupts at the surface. When two plates move apart, a spreading ridge—a chain of gentle volcanoes—is formed. Where plates collide, one is forced beneath the other to form a subduction zone. The sinking plate partly melts and the hot liquid magma rises to feed volcanoes just inside the plate boundary. A third kind of volcano erupts above a hot spot, an active center in Earth's mantle.

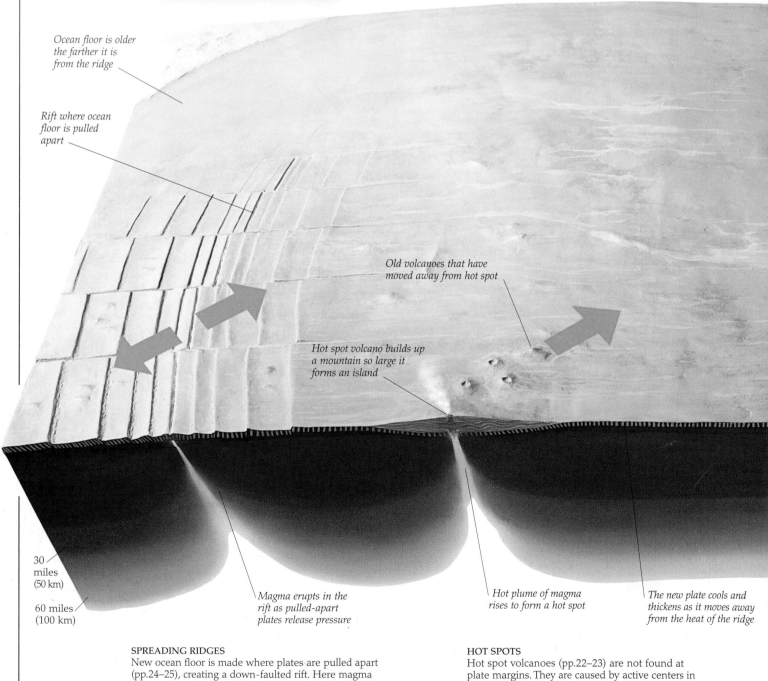

Ocean floor is older the farther it is from the ridge

Rift where ocean floor is pulled apart

Old volcanoes that have moved away from hot spot

Hot spot volcano builds up a mountain so large it forms an island

30 miles (50 km)

60 miles (100 km)

Magma erupts in the rift as pulled-apart plates release pressure

Hot plume of magma rises to form a hot spot

The new plate cools and thickens as it moves away from the heat of the ridge

SPREADING RIDGES
New ocean floor is made where plates are pulled apart (pp.24–25), creating a down-faulted rift. Here magma rises and erupts as lava through fissures and vents. Continued rifting produces successive new rifts and separates the parallel, flanking ridges—each one older than the next. All the ocean floor has been made this way in the last 200 million years.

HOT SPOTS
Hot spot volcanoes (pp.22–23) are not found at plate margins. They are caused by active centers in the mantle that produce huge volumes of magma. The magma rises to the surface and punches a hole in the plate, forming a volcano. Because the hot spot in the mantle stays still while the plate moves over it, the hot spot seems to drift across the plate.

VOLCANO CHAIN
Guatemala in Central America is home to a chain of volcanoes, many still active. They sit on top of a subduction zone formed as the Cocos Plate sinks beneath the larger North American Plate.

FINDING FAULT
The San Andreas fault zone is probably the most famous plate boundary in the world. It is easy to see the direction of movement from rivers and roads, even whole mountain ranges that have been split apart by the relentless sideways sliding.

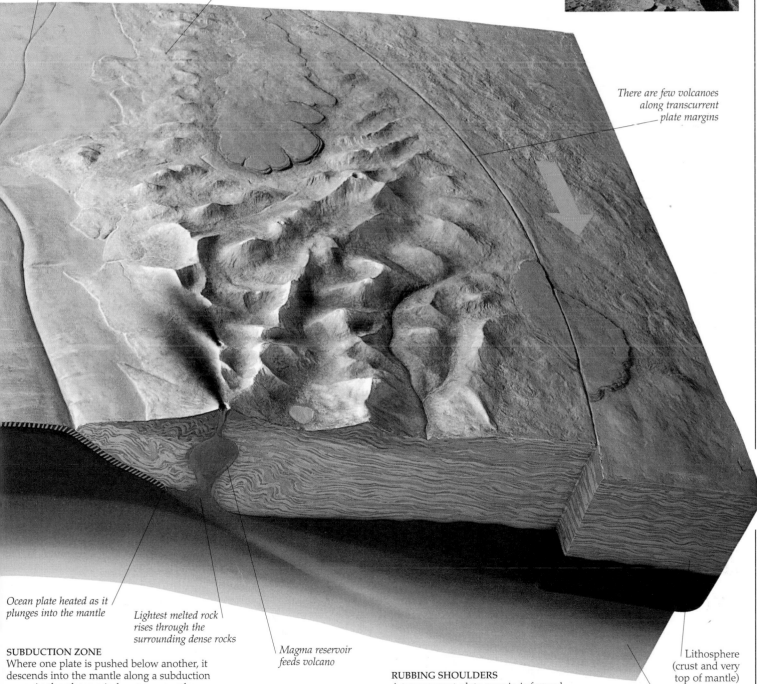

A deep ocean trench is formed where the ocean floor descends in a subduction zone

Continental margin thickened and lifted above subduction zone

There are few volcanoes along transcurrent plate margins

Ocean plate heated as it plunges into the mantle

Lightest melted rock rises through the surrounding dense rocks

Magma reservoir feeds volcano

Lithosphere (crust and very top of mantle)

Asthenosphere (soft, upper part of mantle)

SUBDUCTION ZONE
Where one plate is pushed below another, it descends into the mantle along a subduction zone. As the plates grind past one another, earthquakes are generated, some very large. Deep down, the friction melts some rocks to form magma. This liquid magma rises to feed volcanoes within the margin of the plate above (pp.14–15).

RUBBING SHOULDERS
A transcurrent plate margin is formed where two plates meet at an odd angle. The resulting boundary is called a transcurrent fault zone. Large earthquakes occur when the fault sticks, then suddenly slips.

When a mountain explodes

THE MOST SPECTACULAR AND DESTRUCTIVE eruptions occur at
volcanoes by subduction zones (pp.10–13). These volcanoes
may lie dormant for many centuries between eruptions
(pp.38–39). When they do explode, the eruption can be
extraordinarily violent. When Mount St. Helens, a volcano in
the Cascade Range of the Pacific Northwest, blew its top on
May 18, 1980, it had been quiet for 123 years. The huge explosion
that decapitated the mountain was heard in Vancouver, Canada, 200 miles
(320 km) to the north. The north side of the mountain was pulverized and
blown out over the surrounding forest. This avalanche of rock was
quickly overtaken by clouds of newly erupted ash. These became
pyroclastic flows (p.16), flows of hot ash and gas that rushed down
the steep slopes of the volcano at terrifying speeds, incinerating
everything they met. The explosion continued for nine hours,
lofting millions of tons of ash 15 miles (22 km) up into the
atmosphere. Mud flows choked the river valleys with a
mixture of ash, ice, and uprooted trees (pp.56–57).
Vast areas of forest were flattened by
the blast, and 57 people, including
volcanologist David Johnston,
were killed.

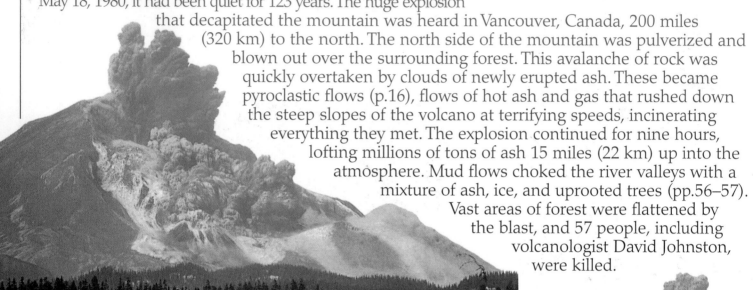

38 SECONDS AFTER THE FIRST EXPLOSION
After two months of small earthquakes and explosions, the north slope of
Mount St. Helens had grown a huge bulge. At 8:32 a.m. on May 18, 1980,
the whole north side suddenly shivered and seemed to turn to liquid. As the
pressure inside the volcano was reduced, the hot magma down below began to
froth and explode. This picture, taken 38 seconds into the explosion, shows the
avalanche roaring down the north face. Just above the avalanche, a cloud of
ash and gas is blasting skyward.

Ashy eruption cloud

Feeder pipe

*Reservoir of hot,
gassy magma*

FEEDING THE FURY
Lighter than the solid rock around it, hot magma had
risen under Mount St. Helens. The magma was melt
from old oceanic plate consumed in the subduction
zone off the coast (pp.12–13). It had gathered in an
underground pool, the magma reservoir. The hot rock
reached the crater along a feeder pipe, which took on
the shape of a gun barrel as the eruption progressed.

FOUR SECONDS LATER...
...the avalanche of old rock has been overtaken by the darker,
growing cloud of ash, which contains newly erupted material.
Gary Rosenquist, who took these pictures, said later that "the
sight... was so overwhelming that I became dizzy and had to turn
away to keep my balance." From his viewpoint 11 miles (18 km)
away, he didn't hear a sound through the whole blast.

MOVING WALL OF ASH

As the ash cloud blasted out beyond the flanks of the volcano, it became lighter than air and began to rise. Gary Rosenquist took this last picture before he ran for his car. "The turbulent cloud loomed behind us as we sped down Road 99," he wrote later. "We raced toward Randle as marble-sized mudballs flattened against the windshield. Minutes later it was completely dark. We groped through the choking ash cloud to safety."

LAST GASP

In the months after the big eruption, the diminishing pressure in the magma reservoir pushed up thick, pasty lava. The sticky rock was squeezed out like toothpaste from a tube. It formed a bulging dome, which reached a height of 800 ft (260 m) in 1986. At one point, a spine of stiff lava grew out of the dome. Like the bigger spine pushed up by Mount Pelée in 1902 (pp.32–33), this eventually crumbled to a heap of lava fragments.

TREE-REMOVAL ZONE

Mature forests of trees up to 150 ft (50 m) tall were flattened by the blast of the eruption. Closest to the mountain, in the "tree-removal zone," the ground was scoured of virtually everything.

ELEVEN SECONDS LATER...

... the avalanche of old rock has been completely overtaken by the faster blast of ash. On the right, huge chunks of airborne rock can be clearly seen as they are catapulted out of the cloud.

Ash and dust

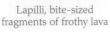

Lapilli, bite-sized fragments of frothy lava

Ash, smaller pyroclastic fragments

Dust, the smallest, lightest lava fragments

THE MOST EXPLOSIVE VOLCANOES pour clouds of ash high into the sky. The ash is formed because gas dissolved in the magma escapes with such force that it blasts the hot rock into billions of tiny pieces. The resulting rock fragments are collectively known as pyroclastics. They range from lava blocks as big as houses (p.18) to powdery dust fine enough to float around the world in the upper atmosphere (pp.34–35). Between these two extremes are lapilli (Latin for "little stones") and ash. Very powerful explosive eruptions can hurl huge blocks several miles from the volcano. But the biggest fragments usually land closest to the vent, while the smallest ones are flung the farthest. In some eruptions, the ash clouds collapse under their own weight, forming pyroclastic flows. Unlike lava flows, pyroclastic flows can be extremely dangerous. Many of the worst volcanic disasters have been caused by pyroclastic flows or pyroclastic surges, flows containing more hot gas than ash.

CONSTRUCTING A CONE
Mountains are built up as pyroclastics burst from the crater and settle layer upon layer on a volcano's slopes. Gassy fire-fountain eruptions build cinder cones of bombs and ash. These cinder cones are two of several in a crater in Maui, Hawaii (pp.22–23).

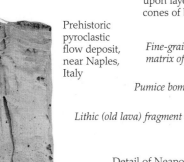

Prehistoric pyroclastic flow deposit, near Naples, Italy

Fine-grained matrix of ash

Pumice bomb

Lithic (old lava) fragment

Detail of Neapolitan pyroclastic flow deposit

VOLCANO BIOGRAPHY
Frozen in a volcano's slopes is a detailed history of its past eruptions. The rock layers, formed as falling ash cooled and hardened, can be dated and their textures and structures analyzed. The ash layers in this cross-section were erupted by a volcano about 500 million years ago.

GLOWING AVALANCHES
If the erupted mixture of hot rocks and gas is heavier than air, it may flow downhill at more than 60 mph (100 km/h). Such a pyroclastic flow (also called an ash flow, *nuée ardente*, or glowing avalanche) may flatten everything in its path. Equally destructive are pyroclastic surges, flows that contain more hot gas than ash. The residents of Pompeii (pp.26–30) and Saint-Pierre (pp.32–33) were killed by searing pyroclastic surges.

Long night of the ash cloud

After lying dormant for 600 years, Mount Pinatubo in the Philippines began erupting in June 1991. Huge clouds of ash were thrown into the air, blocking out the sunlight for days. The airborne ash slowly settled out, burying fields and villages for miles around. Over 330 ft (100 m) of ash lay in drifts on the upper slopes of the volcano. Torrential rains followed, causing mud flows that cascaded down the river valleys and swept away roads, bridges, and several villages (p.56). At least 400 people were killed and another 400,000 were left homeless. With no breathing masks to protect themselves from the gritty ash, many of the survivors developed pneumonia. At the very least, their eyes were badly inflamed by the ashy air.

Their fields buried in ash, farmers take their buffalo and head for greener pastures

BREATHING EASY
Every step raises fine ash that fills the air. Covering mouth and nose with a wet cloth helps to keep the throat and lungs clear.

BURIED CROPS
A thin fall of ash fertilizes the soil (pp.40–41), but too much destroys crops. With no water to wash off the abrasive powder, this corn is inedible. Whole harvests were lost in the heavy ash falls that followed the eruptions of Mount Pinatubo.

Fiery rocks

VOLCANOES ERUPT red-hot lava. Sometimes the lava oozes gently from a hole in the ground. At other times it is thrown into the air in spectacular fire fountains, running together again as it lands. Either way, the lava flows off in rivers of hot rock that may spread out and cover the countryside before it cools. Fire fountains and lava flows are common in Iceland (pp.24–25) and Hawaii (pp.22–23). They are relatively predictable, and it's often possible to venture near them and photograph them in close-up. But if the lava is less fluid and its supply is variable, explosions occur from time to time as volcanic gas escapes from the hot rock. As the gas content changes, a volcano may switch without warning from one type of eruption to another. Explosions throw out bombs and blocks, chunks of flying lava that litter the ground around the vent. It is dangerous to get close to explosive eruptions because the size and timing of the explosions varies.

REMELTED LAVA
Some of the gas dissolved in lava is lost when it erupts and cools. This piece of once-cold lava was reheated and remelted in a special oven. It frothed up, showing that it still contained much of its original gas.

Dense round bomb

A red iron oxide covers this bomb thrown out by Mount Etna, on the island of Sicily in Italy (pp.6–7)

BOMBS AND BLOCKS
Bombs and blocks can be as big as houses or as small as tennis balls. Bombs are usually more rounded, while blocks are more dense and angular. Their shapes depend upon how molten or gassy the lava was during flight. Very liquid chunks of lava plop to the ground like cow pies; denser, more solid ones thud or shatter as they land. Both bombs and blocks draw long, fiery traces when they are photographed at night with a long time exposure.

Small, explosive eruption photographed at night on Mount Etna

A TWISTED TAIL
The odd twists and tails of many bombs are formed as they spin through the air.

HAWAIIAN AA
Glowing red at night, the intense heat of an aa flow shows through the surface crust of cooling lava. The flow moves forward like a bulldozer track, as scoria blocks drop down the advancing front and are run over. Lava flows cool very slowly because rock is a poor conductor of heat. As they harden, the flows slow down and grow thicker.

Hardened chunk of ropy pahoehoe lava

PAHOEHOE FLOWS
Pahoehoe is more fluid than aa and contains more gas. As its surface cools, the flow grows a thin, pliable skin. The hot lava on the inside distorts the skin, wrinkling it so its surface looks like the coils of a rope. The crust may grow so thick that people can walk across it while red-hot lava continues to flow in a tunnel below (p.23). The hot lava may remelt the overlying crust, which drips off. Kept hot by tunnels, pahoehoe lava can flow as far as villages on the volcano's lower slopes.

Aa and pahoehoe

Lava flows pose little danger to people as they rarely travel faster than a few miles an hour. The two kinds of flows get their names from Hawaiian words. Aa (pronounced *ah-ah*) flows are covered in sharp, angular chunks of lava known as scoria. This makes them difficult to walk over when they have cooled, unlike pahoehoe (*pa-hoy-hoy*) flows, which grow a smooth skin soon after they leave the vent. The chilled surface traps gas, keeping flows hot and mobile. Pahoehoe flows are rarely more than 3 ft (1 m) thick, while the thickest aa flows may be 330 ft (100 m) deep.

Driblets of remelted lava from the roof of a pahoehoe tunnel

SPINY AND TWISTED
This chunk of scoria from the surface of an aa flow was twisted as it was carried along.

PAHOEHOE TOE
This picture shows red-hot pahoehoe bulging through a crack in its own skin. New skin is forming over the bulge. A pahoehoe flow creeps forward with thousands of little breakouts like this one.

FIRE AND WATER
Volcanic islands like Hawaii and Iceland are usually fringed by black beaches. The sand is formed when hot lava hits the sea and is shattered into tiny, glassy particles. It is black because the lava is rich in dark minerals like iron oxides and low in light-colored ones like quartz.

Black sand from the volcanic island of Santorini in Greece

Gas and lightning

Captain Haddock and friends flee from a volcano's sulfurous gases in the Tintin adventure *Flight 71.4. for Sydney*

VOLCANIC GASES ARE EXTREMELY DANGEROUS. In August 1986, a small explosion in Lake Nyos in Cameroon, Central Africa, signaled the release of a cloud of volcanic gases. The poisonous fumes killed 1,700 people living in villages below the lake. The main killer in the cloud was carbon dioxide, a heavy gas that flows downhill and gathers in hollows.

Carbon dioxide is particularly dangerous because it has no odor and is very hard to detect—unlike many volcanic gases, which are extremely smelly. Hydrogen sulfide smells like rotten cabbage, and the acidic gases hydrogen chloride and sulfur dioxide sting the eyes and throat. They also eat through clothes, leaving holes with bleached haloes around them. Hydrogen fluoride, which is very poisonous, is strong enough to etch glass. Early volcano observers who thought they saw flames during eruptions were probably looking at great veils of glowing gases. Flames occur when hydrogen gas catches fire, but they are flimsy and hard to see. More impressive are lightning flashes, which are often seen during ashy eruptions.

RAISING A STINK
Nearly 40 years after the last eruption of Kawah Idjen in Java, Indonesia, sulfur and other gases are still escaping into the volcano's crater. Here, volcanologist Katia Krafft (pp.42–43) collects gas samples from the crater floor.

STEAM-ASSISTED ERUPTION
Water expands enormously when it turns to steam. So when magma meets water, the power of the eruption is orders of magnitude greater. When the new island of Surtsey was formed off Iceland in November 1963 (p.41), sea water poured into the vent and hit the hot magma, producing spectacular explosions and huge clouds of steam.

GAS MASK
Made to protect the wearer against low concentrations of acidic gases, this gas mask also keeps out all but the finest volcanic dust.

Volcanologist studying Hawaiian lava flows behind the safety of a gas mask

LIGHTNING FLASH
Immense flashes of lightning are often seen during eruptions. They are caused by a build up of static electricity produced when the tiny fragments of lava in an ash cloud rub against each other. The electrical charge is released in bolts that leap through the cloud, as they do in a thunderstorm. This picture shows lightning bolts at Mount Tolbachik in Kamchatka, Siberia. It was taken during the day—the Sun can be seen on the far left, shining feebly through a cloud of dust and gas.

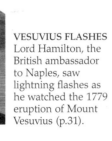

VESUVIUS FLASHES
Lord Hamilton, the British ambassador to Naples, saw lightning flashes as he watched the 1779 eruption of Mount Vesuvius (p.31).

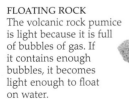

FLOATING ROCK
The volcanic rock pumice is light because it is full of bubbles of gas. If it contains enough bubbles, it becomes light enough to float on water.

FLOATING ON AN ACID LAKE
Volcanologists sample volcanic gases on the surface of an acid lake in the crater of Kawah Idjen. The gases rising from the volcano are dissolved in the lake water which fills much of the crater. Such acid lakes are very hostile to life, and would devour a swimmer's skin in minutes.

Hot spots

THE LARGEST VOLCANOES ON EARTH are above hot spots.
Two of the biggest, Mauna Loa and Kilauea, are on the
island of Hawaii. The Hawaiian island chain is the tip
of a huge undersea mountain range that has built up
over millions of years as the hot spot erupted great
volumes of lava onto the moving plate above it. Hot
spots are randomly distributed, and have little if any
relation to today's plate boundaries (pp.12–15). Some
geologists believe that certain hot spots relate to old
plate boundary positions. Fractures that were part of the
old boundary system still act as channels for magma to
escape to the surface. This reduces the pressure on the
mantle, which in turn stimulates further melting, making
more magma to feed the hot spot. Other hot spots may
be initiators of new plate boundaries. Iceland is a hot
spot 1,200 miles (2,000 km) across. If it weren't for this
huge volcanic structure buoying it up, much of
northwest Europe would be below sea level.

MAUNA LOA ERUPTS
During one of the longest eruptions
on Hawaii, Mauna Loa was active
at the same time as the younger
volcano Kilauea. Here, fire
fountains have built a black
cinder cone (p.16). Hot, very
liquid pahoehoe lava has
undermined one side of the
cone, which has collapsed.

VOLCANO GODDESS
Some Hawaiians believe that the powerful
goddess Pele makes mountains, melts rocks,
destroys forests, and builds new islands.
The fiery goddess is said to live in the crater
Halema'uma'u, at the summit of Kilauea
volcano on the island of Hawaii.

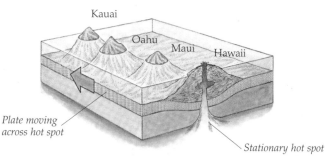

Kauai

Oahu

Maui

Hawaii

*Plate moving
across hot spot*

Stationary hot spot

A STRING OF ISLANDS
The Pacific Plate is moving over the stationary Hawaiian
hot spot, which is presently under the south end of the
island of Hawaii. There are two active volcanoes, Mauna
Loa and Kilauea, on Hawaii, and a third, Loihi, is growing
below the sea to the south. The north end of the island of
Hawaii is made up of older, extinct volcanoes, and a string
of progressively older volcanic islands lies to the northwest.

PELE'S HAIR
The hot, fluid lava of a Hawaiian fire fountain may be blown into fine, glassy strands. These are known as Pele's hair.

WANDERING HOT SPOT
Hot-spot volcanoes erupt often and are relatively easy to get close to and photograph. This is Piton de la Fournaise on the island of Réunion in the Indian Ocean (p.11). The island is the tip of a huge volcano that rises 4 miles (7 km) above the ocean floor. The hot spot has moved 2,500 miles (4,000 km) in the last 30 million years.

Lava has solidified around this tree, leaving a tree mold

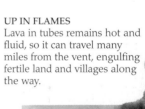

Road buried by lava during eruption of Kilauea

UP IN FLAMES
Lava in tubes remains hot and fluid, so it can travel many miles from the vent, engulfing fertile land and villages along the way.

LAVA TUBE
The skin of a pahoehoe flow may crust over into a roof thick enough to walk on. Only a yard or so below, hot lava continues to run in a tunnel or "tube." Occasional collapses in the roof provide a window through which the flowing lava can be watched and measured. Hot lava dripping off the underside of the roof creates strange formations called lava stalagmites and stalactites.

Lava stalagmite made of drips in a pahoehoe tube

Spreading ridges

THE ROCKS THAT MAKE up the ocean floor are all young—nowhere older than 200 million years. This is because new ocean plate is constantly being made by volcanic eruptions deep below the ocean waters. A long range of mountains snakes through the oceans, cut at its heart by a rift valley. The volcanoes in this rift valley erupt constantly, producing new volcanic rock. Under the huge pressure of the ocean water, the lava erupts gently, like toothpaste squeezed from a tube, to form rounded shapes known as pillow lava. The new rock fills in the widening rift as the plates pull apart. In this way the oceans grow just a little wider, a fraction of an inch per year. In places, the rifts are bubbling with volcanic hot springs— black smokers—that exude water rich in metal sulfides. First discovered in 1977, black smokers are the subject of intense research. They are home to life-forms found nowhere else on the planet.

RIFT THROUGH ICELAND
In Iceland, geologists can study ridges without getting wet. This is the Skaftar fissure, part of a 16-mile- (27-km-) long rift that opened in 1783, erupting 3 cubic miles (13 cubic km) of lava over eight months. The dust and gas killed 75 percent of the animals in Iceland, and 10,000 Icelanders died in the famine that followed.

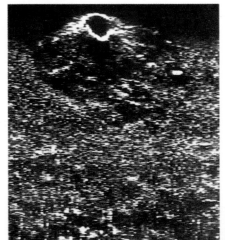

UNDERSEA VOLCANO
A long-range side-scan sonar known as GLORIA created this image of a volcano 13,000 ft (4,000 m) below the Pacific Ocean. The submarine volcano is 6 miles (10 km) across.

Icelandic eruptions give a glimpse of how spreading ridges make new oceanic plate. The eruptions tend to be from long cracks, rather than central craters.

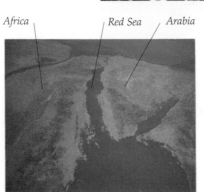

Africa   *Red Sea*   *Arabia*

SPLITTING CONTINENT
A spreading ridge runs through the Red Sea. For the last 20 million years it has been making new ocean floor, as Arabia moves away from Africa.

Submersible *Alvin*, which took photos of mid-ocean ridges

DEEP-SEA SHRIMP
This new species of
shrimp was found at the
Galápagos Rift in the
Pacific Ocean in 1979.

Black smokers

These hot springs are found along spreading
ridges in spots where the ridges are particularly active. The water they pour forth is hot,
acidic, and black with sulfides of copper,
lead, and zinc. These valuable metal
minerals come from the new oceanic
plate that is formed at the ridges. They
are dissolved out by sea water
percolating through
the cooling rock.

*Sulfur-eating tube
worms from the
Galápagos Rift*

Rounded pillow shapes typical of lava erupted
underwater

LIVING WITHOUT SUNLIGHT
The many strange life-forms
found around black smokers
live off microbes that, in turn,
are nourished by mineral-eating
microbes. These urchins were
seen on the Galápagos Rift.

MANGANESE NODULES
The ocean floor is carpeted with black lumps rich in
manganese and other metals. If a way of collecting
them from deep water can be found, these nodules
may become a valuable source of minerals.

Plume of black metal sulfides   *Black smoker chimney*

*Feeder
channel
or pipe*

*Cold sea water
percolating
through hot rock*

Model of
black smoker

Magma reservoir

**LAVA
FEEDER CHANNELS**
Two ancient lava feeder channels
can be seen in the rock above.

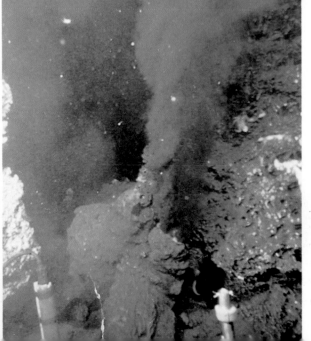

CHIMNEY PIPES
Chilled suddenly as
they meet cold ocean
water, the metal sulfides
crystallize out to form
the chimney pipes that
surround the mouths
of black smokers. These
grow steadily, collapsing
only when they get
too tall.

*Coarse crystal structure
indicates slow cooling*

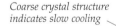

Gabbro, a coarsely crystalline rock from an
old sea-floor magma reservoir in Cyprus

The great eruption of Vesuvius

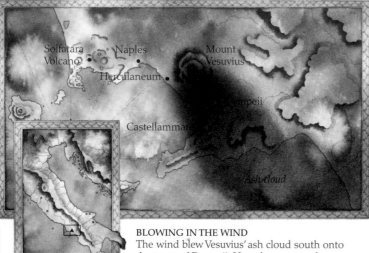

PLINY THE YOUNGER
This scholar watched the eruption cloud from across the Bay of Naples, where he was staying with his uncle, Pliny the Elder.

PERHAPS THE MOST FAMOUS ERUPTION of all time shook Mount Vesuvius near Naples in Italy in 79 CE. When the long-dormant volcano erupted on August 24, the residents of the Roman towns of Pompeii and Herculaneum were caught unawares. Hot ash and lapilli rained down on Pompeii for hours until it was buried several yards deep. Many people escaped, coughing and stumbling through the darkness of the ash cloud. Those caught in the town were overwhelmed by a sudden powerful blast of ash and gas (a pyroclastic surge, p.16). The apocalyptic events were described in detail by Pliny the Younger. His famous letters to Tacitus are the first known eyewitness account of a volcanic eruption. The buried towns were virtually forgotten until excavations began in the 18th century. The digs have since unearthed a priceless archeological and geological treasure, two thriving Roman towns frozen in the moments of their destruction.

BLOWING IN THE WIND
The wind blew Vesuvius' ash cloud south onto the town of Pompeii. Herculaneum, to the west of the volcano, was hardly touched by falling ash. But the pyroclastic flows and surges (p.16) that followed flowed downhill in all directions, covering both towns.

BEWARE OF DOG
This floor mosaic from a Pompeii entranceway was meant to warn off intruders. A similar mosaic says *cave canem*—Latin for "beware of the dog."

Modern Italian bread

BURNED TO A CRISP
This carbonized loaf of bread was one of several found in the brick oven of a bakery. The baker's stamp can still be seen, nearly 2,000 years after the day the bread was baked.

Flour mill made of lava, a tough rock also used to pave streets

Portrait of a poet or princess, detail of a floor mosaic found at Pompeii

Bowl of preserved eggs

SNAKE CHARM
Fine gold and silver jewelry, some set with emeralds, was found in the buried town. This hollow bracelet in the shape of a coiled snake is made of thick gold. Certain styles were abundant. Over 80 copies of one kind of earring were found, suggesting mass-production of popular models.

Fresh walnuts

Fresh figs, still grown on the slopes of Vesuvius

Bowl of carbonized figs

Carbonized food

Organic compounds like wood, bone, and food contain carbon. Normally they would burn when heated. But in some circumstances, the hot ash and gas stopped oxygen from combining with the carbon, so that the compounds turned to charcoal instead. This process, called carbonization, left the fine details of many foodstuffs perfectly preserved in the fine ash.

Bowl of carbonized walnuts

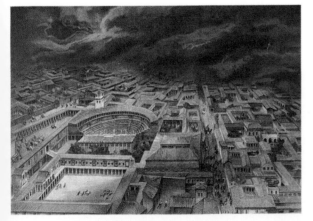

PANIC IN THE STREETS
The large theater (the open, semicircular building) and the gladiator's gymnasium (in front of the theater) can be seen in this artist's impression of the destruction of Pompeii. In the crowded streets, stragglers are running for their lives from the menacing black clouds.

DEATH OF PLINY THE ELDER
In one letter, Pliny the Younger wrote of his uncle and another official fleeing with "pillows tied upon their heads with napkins; and this was their whole defense against the storm of stones that fell around them. It was now day everywhere else, but there a deeper darkness prevailed than in the thickest night… my uncle … raised himself up with the assistance of two of his servants, and instantly fell down dead; suffocated, as I conjecture, by some gross and noxious vapor… his body was found entire… looking more like a man asleep than dead."

Continued on next page

THE FAITHFUL DOG
This guard dog found at the house of Vesonius Primus died at his post, still tethered by a chain attached to his bronze collar.

Caught in the act of dying

Over 2,000 people died in Pompeii when the eruption of Mount Vesuvius overwhelmed the Roman town. We know about these Roman citizens from plaster casts that show them at the moment of their death. As the fleeing Pompeiians died, the rain of ash and pumice set around their bodies rather like wet cement. With time, the soft body parts decayed and the ash and pumice turned to solid rock. The shapes of the dead Romans' bodies were left as hollows in the rock. Only the hard bones remained inside the hollows. In 1860, the Italian king appointed Giuseppe Fiorelli as director of the excavations. Fiorelli started the first systematic, large-scale excavations of the ancient city. He also invented a method for removing the skeletons from the body hollows and filling the space with wet plaster of Paris. After the plaster hardened, a true representation of the bodies could be dug out of the volcanic rock. Many of these startling casts show people grimacing, trying to hide, or huddling together in terror. Excavations at Pompeii continue today, and Fiorelli's method is still used whenever new bodies are unearthed. It has also been used to make casts of animals, trees, doors, furniture, and cart wheels.

Body cavity is discovered

Cavity is filled with wet plaster of Paris

LAST DAY OF POMPEII
Fascinated by the apocalyptic stories of Pompeii, many artists have depicted its destruction. Like most, this painting by 19th-century German artist Karl Bruillov is rather fanciful. He has shown flames as houses catch fire.

Cast of suffocated baby, found in the Garden of the Fugitives

SHROUD OF DEATH
His body cast shows the folds of the clothing this man was wearing when he died. He is clutching his chest, indicating his pain in breathing. Most of the victims are believed to have died of suffocation.

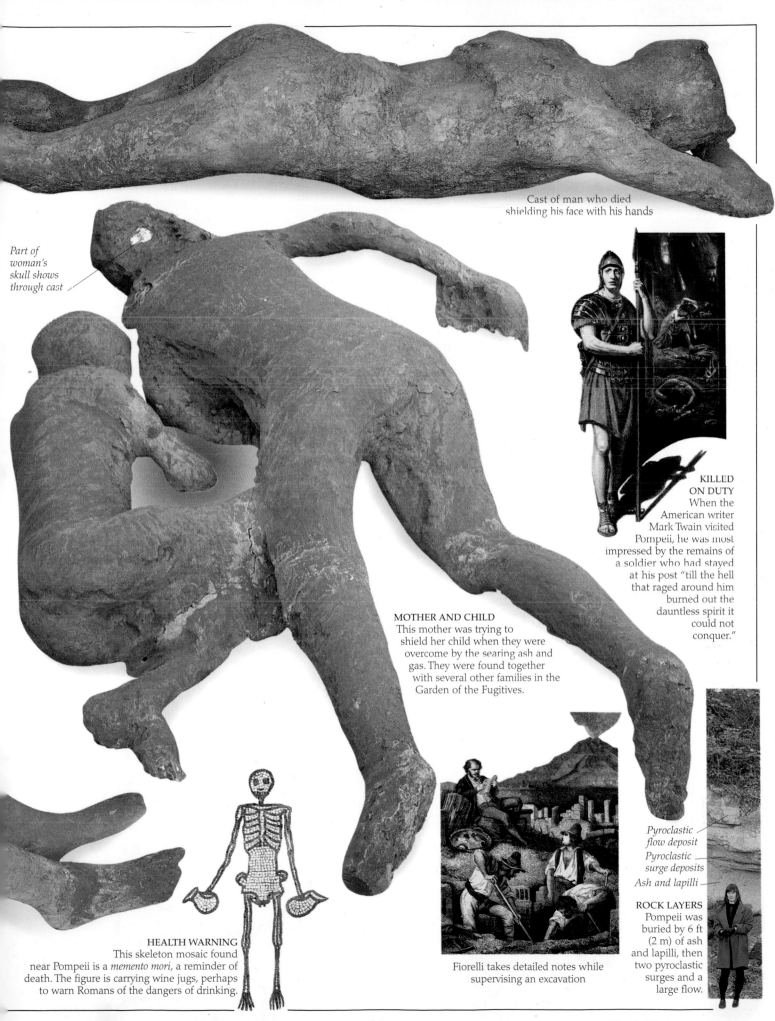

Cast of man who died shielding his face with his hands

Part of woman's skull shows through cast

KILLED ON DUTY
When the American writer Mark Twain visited Pompeii, he was most impressed by the remains of a soldier who had stayed at his post "till the hell that raged around him burned out the dauntless spirit it could not conquer."

MOTHER AND CHILD
This mother was trying to shield her child when they were overcome by the searing ash and gas. They were found together with several other families in the Garden of the Fugitives.

HEALTH WARNING
This skeleton mosaic found near Pompeii is a *memento mori*, a reminder of death. The figure is carrying wine jugs, perhaps to warn Romans of the dangers of drinking.

Fiorelli takes detailed notes while supervising an excavation

Pyroclastic flow deposit
Pyroclastic surge deposits
Ash and lapilli

ROCK LAYERS
Pompeii was buried by 6 ft (2 m) of ash and lapilli, then two pyroclastic surges and a large flow.

29

Continued on next page

Herculaneum

In 79 CE, the Roman town of Herculaneum was a luxurious seaside resort. When Mount Vesuvius began to erupt on August 24, the great ash cloud that engulfed Pompeii missed Herculaneum (p.26). Less than 1 in (3 cm) of debris had fallen on the town when it was blasted by a great surge of hot ash and gas. Early excavations uncovered very few bodies, which was puzzling. Archeologists decided that most of the inhabitants must have escaped in boats before the surge. But in the 1980s, several hundred skeletons were found huddled beneath massive brick arches that once stood on the shoreline. A great crowd of Herculaneans must have taken shelter there, only to be overcome by the deadly waves of ash and gas.

NEPTUNE AND AMPHITRITE
This mosaic of two mythological figures was unearthed in the courtyard of a wealthy wine merchant's house in Herculaneum.

WALKING IN THE RUINS
The excavations of the Roman town have created a deep hole that is surrounded by the modern city of Herculaneum (p.60). These visitors to the ruins are walking on a street laid with lava paving stones.

ROMAN SKELETONS
Unlike the bones found in Pompeii, the skeletons from Herculaneum have no surrounding body shape. This is because the ground they lay in was waterlogged. As the bodies decayed, the wet ash nestled closer and closer until it was packed tightly around the bones.

A TOMB OF HOT ROCK
Herculaneum was hit by six pyroclastic surges (p.16–17). Each one was followed by a thick flow of hot ash, pumice, and rock. The flows buried the town in 65 ft (20 m) of volcanic debris—five times more than covered the neighboring town of Pompeii.

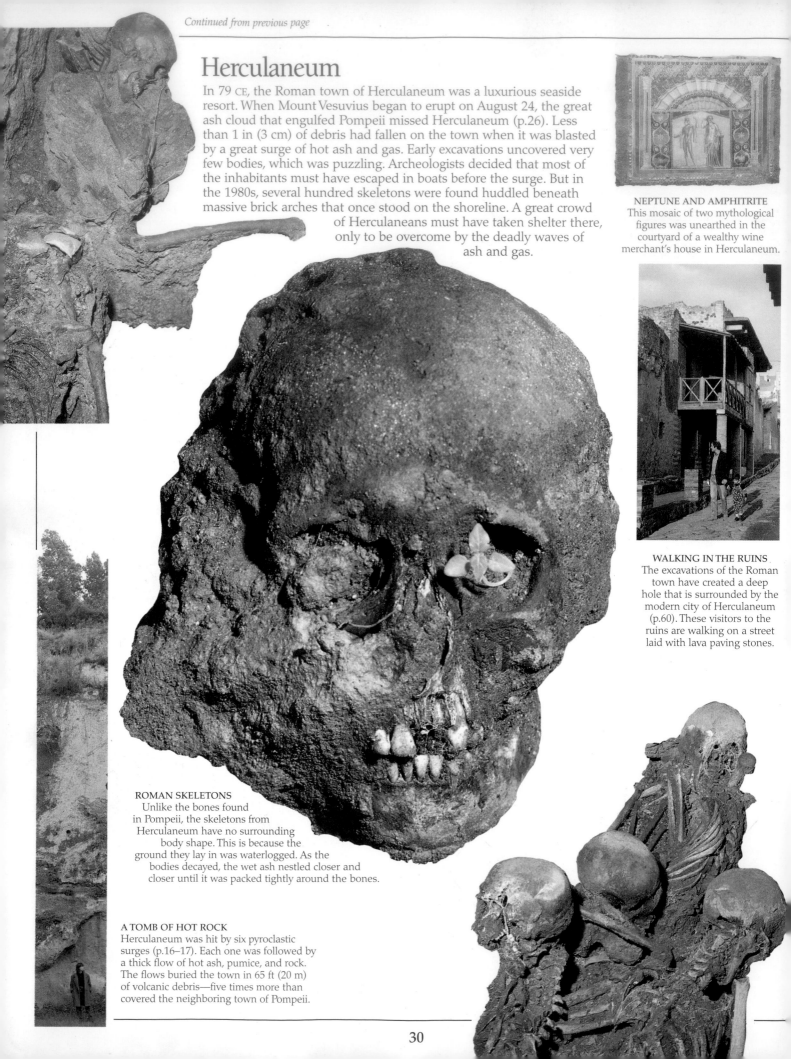

TEXTBOOK ERUPTION
This 1767 engraving (above), which probably shows the 1760 eruption, was published in Millar's *New Complete & Universal System of Geography*.

1631 eruption (left)

HAMILTON'S VIEW
The British ambassador to Naples, Lord Hamilton (p.21), included this view of the 1779 eruption in his book *The Campi Phlegraei* (which literally means "flaming fields"). The artist is Pietro Fabris (p.39).

The world's most visited volcano

The Romans who lived in the shadow of Vesuvius were scarcely aware that it was a volcano. The mountain had erupted 800 years earlier, but it had been calm since then, and its slopes had grown green and tranquil. Vesuvius was more explosive after 79 CE, erupting numerous times in the 20 centuries since Pompeii and Herculaneum were destroyed. The biggest recent eruption, in 1631, produced pyroclastic surges and flows. Since the 18th century, travelers have flocked to Naples to see the excavations, the art treasures, and the angry mountain. Even today tourists make the difficult climb to the summit and pay to look into the steaming crater.

German etching of 1885 eruption showing fires started by lava flows

ON THE TOURIST MAP
This satirical cartoon shows English tourists at the crater of Vesuvius in 1890. A tourist guide-book of 1883 warns visitors that all "guides" are impostors. It advises sightseers to wear their worst clothes because boots are ruined by the sharp lava and colorful dresses are stained by the sulfur.

Vesuv. Ash rain of the eruption
(March 1944: days 22. 23 24. 25. 26)

TRAVELING IN STYLE
From 1890 to 1944, a funicular railroad carried sightseers up to the crater of Vesuvius. Here, tourists watch the 1933 eruption.

SOUVENIR OF VESUVIUS
Centuries ago, souvenirs from Naples included Roman artifacts stolen from the excavations. These days, security is tighter, and boxes of lava and ash are more common souvenirs. Some of the boxes contain colorful industrial slag instead.

A modern Pompeii

ONE OF THE WORST VOLCANIC DISASTERS of the 20th century happened on May 8, 1902 on the French Caribbean island of Martinique. It was Ascension Day, and most of the inhabitants of Saint-Pierre were ignoring Mount Pelée, the volcano that towered over the city. When it erupted, just before 8 a.m., the mountain sent a cloud of glowing gas down on the picturesque port. Saint-Pierre and all its inhabitants were engulfed. Eyewitnesses on ships in the harbor described the cloud as shriveling and incinerating everything it touched. One said, "The wave of fire was on us and over us like a lightning flash. It sounded like thousands of cannon." Within minutes, Saint-Pierre was charred beyond recognition. The blasted remains bore only a thin coating of ash as witness to the horrific cloud. A few sailors survived on their ships, but all but two of the city's 29,000 residents were killed.

SCARRED SURVIVOR
The heat pitted the surface of this statue. Like many objects, it shows more intense heating on the side facing the volcano—in this case, the far side.

ALFRED LACROIX
French volcanologist Alfred Lacroix arrived in Saint-Pierre on June 23 and spent a year studying Mount Pelée. In his famous report on the eruption, he described the strange *nuées ardentes* or "glowing clouds" that overran Saint-Pierre. Nowadays these would be called pyroclastic flows or surges (p.16).

Broken statuette

WHEN THE CLOCKS STOPPED
This pocket watch was melted to a standstill at 8:15 a.m.

Carbonized spaghetti

Carbonized prune

Ash fragment

Melted medicine bottle

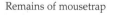

Remains of mousetrap

MELTED GLASS
Like the excavations of Pompeii, the ruins of Saint-Pierre still give up the secrets of the awful event. Discovered in the 1950s, these partially melted objects bear witness to everyday life in a small French colony at the beginning of the 20th century. Some are either so melted or so unfamiliar that it is hard to guess what they are.

Fine volcanic ash melted into glaze

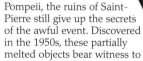

Melted wine bottle

Melted metal fork
(rust occurred after eruption)

Top of charred human
femur (thigh bone)

RUINED CITY
The walls of some buildings were all that was left standing in Saint-Pierre. Rum
distilleries and warehouses exploded in the heat, adding to the destruction.
Many died in the cathedral, where the mass for Ascension Day had just begun.

PROTECTING ANGEL?
This angel figurine, made of
corroded metal, is just recognizable.
Unlike Pompeii and Herculaneum,
no great works of art have been
uncovered in Saint-Pierre.

Heap of glass melted
beyond recognition

Charred mug

Squashed candlestick

PETRIFIED
Wood, bone, ceramics, and most foods
contain carbon. Some of these organic
compounds were scorched or burned
completely. Others were carbonized
(pp.26–27), retaining enough of
their shape to be recognizable.

HOT ENOUGH TO MELT METAL
Some metal objects melted or partly
melted. This heap of iron nails was
fused together. The metal spoon lost
part of its bowl, where the metal
was thinnest. The candlestick was
squashed, probably when the building
it was in collapsed (it shows little sign
of melting). Copper telephone wires
in the town were not melted, so the
cloud must have been a little less than
1,981°F (1,083°C), the melting point
of copper.

*Carbonized
coffee beans*

Heap of fused
iron nails

ETERNAL FIGURE
The wooden cross
was burned right off
this crucifix, leaving
the figure of Jesus with
outstretched arms.

THE BARNUM & BAILEY
GREATEST SHOW ON EARTH

LUDGER SYLBARIS

THE ONLY LIVING OBJECT THAT SURVIVED IN THE "SILENT CITY OF DEATH" WHERE 40,000 HUMAN BEINGS
WERE SUFFOCATED, BURNED OR BURIED BY ONE BELCHING BLAST OF MONT PELÉE'S TERRIBLE VOLCANIC ERUPTION

Melted metal spoon

Fused coins

OUT OF THE FRYING PAN
One of the two people left alive in Saint-Pierre was Auguste
Ciparis. A prisoner condemned to death, he survived because
his cell had thick walls with one tiny window that faced away
from the volcano. He was later pardoned and went on to tour
the world as a circus act under the name of Ludger Sylbaris.

Affecting the world's weather

EARLY EARTH
About 4 billion years ago, Earth had no atmosphere and its surface was covered with erupting volcanoes. All the water in the oceans and many of the gases that make up the atmosphere have been produced by volcanoes erupting over the millennia.

A BIG ASHY VOLCANIC ERUPTION has a dramatic effect on the weather. Dark days, severe winds, and heavy falls of rain or even mud may plague the local area for months. If the gas and dust are lofted high into the atmosphere, they may travel great distances around the globe. When this happens, the climate of the whole planet can be altered. The volcanic material filters out some sunlight, reducing temperatures down below. The high-flung particles also affect our views of the Sun and Moon by scattering sunlight of certain frequencies while allowing other wavelengths through. This can cause spectacular sunrises and sunsets. The sun and moon may seem to be wrapped in haloes or glow with strange colors. Two big eruptions in 1783 posed problems for later polar explorers, who encountered unusually thick pack ice. In the longer term, volcanic particles may cause global cooling, mass extinctions, or even ice ages.

LITTLE ICE AGE
Two major eruptions in 1783—Skaftar in Iceland (p.24) and Asama in Japan—were followed by very cold winters in Europe and North America.

WHO KILLED T. REX?
The extinction of the dinosaurs remains a mystery. The most likely cause was climate change as a result of a major asteroid impact and massive volcanic eruptions that occurred simultaneously around 65 million years ago.

VOLCANIC SUNSETS
In 186 CE, the Chinese noted unusually red sunrises and sunsets. These were caused by volcanic emissions from the huge eruption of Mount Taupo in New Zealand. This sunset was caused by dust from the 1980 eruption of nearby Mount St. Helens.

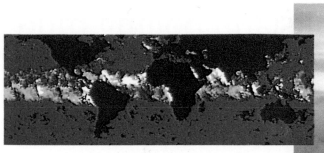

FLOATING AROUND THE GLOBE
The June 1991 eruptions of Mount Pinatubo in the Philippines (right and p.17) spewed ash and gas into the stratosphere. Satellite images (above) showed that by July 25, the particles had spread around the world.

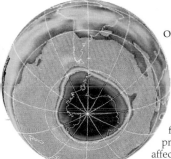

OZONE HOLE
This false-color satellite image shows the hole in the ozone layer over the Antarctic. The sulfur particles that Pinatubo threw high into the atmosphere may cause further damage to this protective layer. This could affect world temperatures.

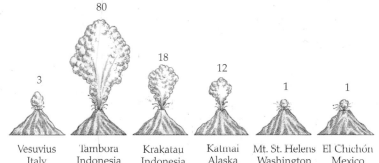

| 80 | 18 | 12 | 1 | 1 |

| Vesuvius Italy 79 CE | Tambora Indonesia 1815 | Krakatau Indonesia 1883 | Katmai Alaska 1912 | Mt. St. Helens Washington 1980 | El Chichón Mexico 1982 |

COMPARING THE SIZE OF ERUPTIONS
The amount of ash a volcano emits is a good measure of the size of the eruption. This diagram compares total emissions of six major eruptions. The units are cubic kilometers. Some large eruptions are relatively unknown. Mount Katmai covered remote parts of Alaska with huge quantities of ash in 1912, and the massive Tambora eruption of 1815 killed more than 90,000 Indonesians. Mount Pinatubo erupted 7 cubic km of ash in 1991.

An artist's impression of the 1883 eruption of Krakatau, Indonesia

ONCE IN A BLUE MOON
In 1883, the Indonesian island of Krakatau (or Krakatoa) was literally blown to pieces in a cataclysmic eruption (p.57). The explosion, one of the loudest ever recorded, was heard 2,400 miles (4,000 km) away at Alice Springs in Australia. Dust and gas colored sunsets in Europe, where the moon and the sun even appeared to be blue or green. Floating islands of pumice drifted across the Indian Ocean for months afterward, causing a great hazard to ships. This piece was washed up on a beach in Madagascar, 4,200 miles (7,000 km) away.

Steam vents and boiling mud

WHERE VOLCANIC HEAT WARMS an area, the water in the ground is heated too. During long dormant periods, the hot water may shoot to the surface in geysers, steam vents, hot springs, and pools of bubbling mud. These hydrothermal (hot water) features make for spectacular scenery in places as far apart as Japan, New Zealand, Iceland, Italy, and the US. The hot water can also be harnessed to do useful work, provided it is not too acidic and its flow is constant. Steam can be directed to spin turbines and generate electricity. In Iceland, hot groundwater is piped into cities, where it is used to heat homes and greenhouses. Many active volcanoes also release steam and other gases between eruptions, and changes in their gas emissions may give clues to future eruptions.

VULCAN, GOD OF FIRE
The ancient Romans believed Solfatara volcano near Naples, Italy, was an entrance to the underworld. It was also one of the workshops of the divine blacksmith, Vulcan—hence our word "volcano."

MEASURING EARTH'S HEAT
A thermocouple (p.43) is being used to measure the heat of a steam vent or fumarole in Solfatara crater. Temperatures here rise to 285°F (140°C). Changes in heat and gas emissions can give clues to future eruptions. They are also monitored before the geothermal energy of an area is tapped. Wild swings make the energy hard to harness.

WORKING UP A SWEAT
The fumaroles in Solfatara exude acidic gases as well as steam. This observatory built in the 19th century is being eaten up by fumarole activity. Where the steam emerges in caverns or grottoes, it is believed to have miraculous healing powers. Since Roman times, visitors have been taking steam baths to treat arthritis and respiratory problems, or just to get the rumored benefits of a good sweat.

CRYSTALS OF SULFUR
The sulfur in volcanic gas cools and crystallizes. In the right conditions, the yellow crystals of this nonmetallic element grow large and translucent. These huge crystals are from Sicily, where sulfur has been mined for centuries. Sulfur has many uses, particularly in manufacturing. It is added to rubber to make it more durable in a process named after the Roman fire god—vulcanization.

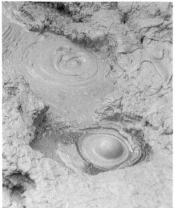

BUBBLING MUD

Some fumaroles bubble up through a mud bath of their own making. The acidic sulfur gases corrode the rock they pass through, creating a great pool (or "pot") of soft mud. The bubbles burst at the surface with strange plopping sounds. The mud in this pot at Solfatara is 140°F (60°C). Some mud pots are much hotter, while others are cool enough for people to wallow in. These mud baths are popular beauty treatments that leave human skin feeling soft and silky.

SMELLY GAS

Spiky growths of sulfur crystals can be clearly seen around this fumarole vent. Close to the vent, the hot, smelly gases are invisible. Like the steam from a teakettle spout, they only show up when the water vapor begins to condense a few inches away.

ROMAN BATHS

The ancient Romans liked the luxury of hot running water and built huge public baths. Baths fed by natural hot springs became medical centers where sick people came to bathe in the mineral-rich water. Many of these spa towns still flourish, and invalids travel great distances to come and "take the waters."

Crust of tiny sulfur crystals from fumarole in Java, Indonesia

Souvenir plate showing Old Faithful geyser (p.7)

HOT WATER POWER

About 40 percent of Iceland's electricity comes from hydrothermal power stations. As the technology improves, this figure is increasing, and other volcanically active countries like Japan, the US, and New Zealand are developing their hydrothermal power programs.

Sleeping beauties

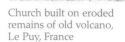

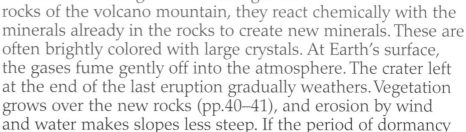

V**OLCANOES SOMETIMES SLEEP** (lie dormant) for years or even centuries between eruptions. In this dormant period, volcanic gases may seep gently from the cooling magma that lies beneath the volcano. As these gases rise through the rocks of the volcano mountain, they react chemically with the minerals already in the rocks to create new minerals. These are often brightly colored with large crystals. At Earth's surface, the gases fume gently off into the atmosphere. The crater left at the end of the last eruption gradually weathers. Vegetation grows over the new rocks (pp.40–41), and erosion by wind and water makes slopes less steep. If the period of dormancy is tens of thousands of years, it may be difficult to recognize that a volcano ever existed. At that stage it may at last be safe to assume that the volcano is extinct.

Church built on eroded remains of old volcano, Le Puy, France

Radiating zeolite crystals from the Faëroe Islands

BORN IN THE LAVA
Zeolite crystals grow in old gas bubbles in lava. They are found in a great variety of colors and forms.

AGATES
These beautiful banded stones form in cavities in cooled or cooling volcanic rocks. The bands, each one formed at a different time, are colored by oxides and hydroxides of iron.

Outer layers of this agate are oldest

Adventurers descend into the crater of Hekla, Iceland, in 1868.

CRATER LAKE
Craters often fill with rainwater between eruptions. This crater lake, on the Shirane volcano in Japan, is very acidic, thanks to gas seeping up from the magma chamber below and dissolving in the water (pp.20–21). During an eruption, the acidic water may be hurled out of the crater. Mixed with hot rock and debris, it could race downhill in a deadly mud flow (pp.56–57).

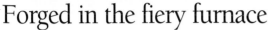

Brightly colored rocks seen
at Solfatara (pp.36–37)
by Lord Hamilton and
illustrated by Pietro Fabris

Cut diamond

Olivine from St. John's Island
in the Red Sea

Forged in the fiery furnace

Hot volcanic fluids concentrate some unusual chemical
elements. These cool slowly inside gas bubbles or other
cavities in the volcanic rock. The slow crystallization
produces large, perfectly-formed crystals that can
be cut and polished into gemstones. The harder
stones are the most prized because they last forever.
Diamond is the hardest stone of all, but softer stones
are valued for their rich colors.

Cut peridot

Uncut diamond in volcanic rock
from the mantle, from Kimberley,
South Africa

RED SEA GEM
Gem-quality olivine is a
deep green color. The gem is
known as peridot.

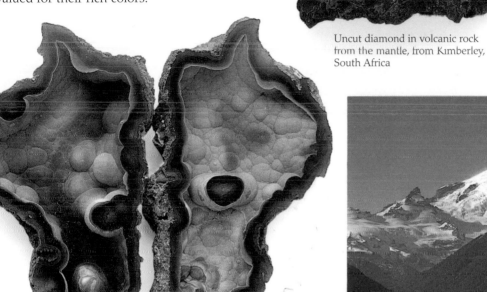

Agate-lined geode (cavity)
from Brazil

BIRTH OF A CALDERA
During a large ashy eruption, the
empty magma chamber may not
be able to support the weight of
the volcano's slopes. These collapse
inward, leaving a huge circular
depression called a caldera. Calderas
may be many miles across.

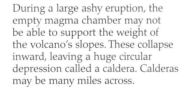

SANTORINI (THERA)
This island is the rim
of a caldera formed by
a huge volcanic eruption
ca. 1620 BCE. The massive
explosion may have led
to the collapse of the
Minoan civilization on
the neighboring island
of Crete. These events
may even be the basis
of the myth of Atlantis,
an island said to have
been destroyed in a
fiery apocalypse.

CASCADE VOLCANO
Mount Rainier is one of a chain of volcanoes in the Cascade Range that
includes Mount St. Helens (pp.14–15). Any of them could become active
again one day. There are no written records, but Mount Rainier probably
erupted several times in the 19th century. These events have been dated
from tree rings, which show a stunting of growth following an eruption.

Life returns to the lava

A VOLCANIC ERUPTION has a profound effect on the landscape. All over the world, the land itself is a priceless resource where crops are grown to feed the population. For the landowner and farmer, an eruption that produces less than 8 in (20 cm) of ash is a blessing. The ash is full of nutrients that enrich the soil. But too much free fertilizer is catastrophic. The worst case for the farmer is when the land is overrun by lava flows. Thick flows can take months to cool. Decades (and in harsh climates even centuries) may pass while mosses and lichens spread slowly across the barren lavascape. Flowering plants and finally trees follow. The upper surface of the solid rock is slowly weathered, and the roots of the plants help to break it down to form soil. Only when a rich soil covers the land is it lush and fertile again. This process may take generations.

1944 lava flow, Mount Vesuvius

Raw lava

Dense, interlocking crystal structure

A few lichens find a home on the lava

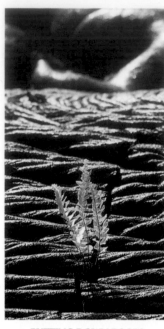

PUTTING DOWN ROOTS
A fern takes root in a ropy pahoehoe lava flow less than a year old on the slopes of Kilauea volcano, Hawaii (pp.22–23).

Lichen covers the lava, providing a soft surface for other organisms

Grasses, often the first flowering plants

Beginnings of topsoil

Lichens cling to exposed parts of rock

GATHERING MOSS
How quickly lava is recolonized by plants depends on the nature of the erupted material. Ashy pyroclastic material is recolonized the fastest. Plants are slowest in taking root on lava flows. The climate and altitude are also important; recolonization is fastest in the tropics. These pieces of lava are all from the same 1944 aa flow on the west slope of Mount Vesuvius in Italy. Some 47 years later, lichen covers a lot of the flow, and moss, grasses, and weedy flowering plants are taking root. The only trees, small pines, were planted by the government.

Rock breaks down to soil, and grass and moss take root

Two species of moss grow in thin soil

New cone is still bare ash

Monte Somma, part of caldera left by huge, prehistoric eruption

Pine forests covers lower slopes

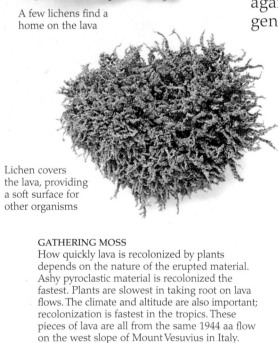

Mount Vesuvius steaming after mild eruption of 1855

BIRTH OF AN ISLAND
In November 1963, an undersea eruption off southwestern Iceland gave birth to a new island, Surtsey (p.20). On the third day (above), eruptions were still highly explosive.

WASHED ASHORE
Seeds blown over or washed up on the beach of Surtsey soon took root in nearby ashfields (above). The beach itself was too harsh for most plants to live on.

LACRIMA CHRISTI
Mount Vesuvius is illustrated on the label of this wine grown on the volcano's slopes. Without the potassium, phosphorus, and other plant nutrients that the volcanic ash brings to the fields, the vines would not grow so thickly and the wine would taste less sweet.

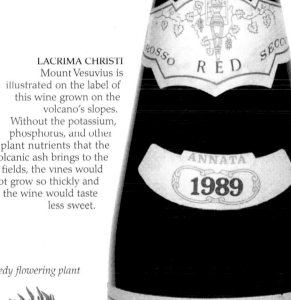

THROUGH THE GRAPEVINE
The lush land around Vesuvius has been fertilized by ash from regular eruptions over the last 20 centuries. The ash supports a large grape harvest, which in turn supports the local wine industry.

Peacock butterfly lives on nectar of flowering plants

Weedy flowering plant

Eventually, soil cover is thick enough to support larger plants.

ROMAN AMPHORAE
The stacks of amphorae for storing wine and olive oil found at Pompeii (pp.26–31) show how fertile the soil was in Roman times.

FLOWER OF LYDIA
This brilliantly colored shrub, a kind of broom, is one of the first plants to grow on the lava at Vesuvius.

Mosaic from Pompeii of Venus, Roman goddess of fertility

Being a volcanologist

FOR A VOLCANOLOGIST—a scientist who watches, records, and interprets volcanoes—life can get uncomfortably hot. Volcanologists spend years monitoring volcanoes to try to predict when and how they will next erupt. Most of their time is spent analyzing data in an office or laboratory, but fieldwork on the slopes of active or erupting volcanoes is vital. This involves taking lava and gas samples and measuring changes in temperature and landforms— sometimes while having to wear protective clothing. Hope of accurate predictions rose in the early 2000s, when scientists identified vibrations, or tremors, lasting a minute or more. They occur when magma forces its way upward through cracks inside the volcano. As their frequency increases, scientists hope to be able to predict the time of an eruption.

KATIA KRAFFT
French volcanologists Katia and Maurice Krafft devoted their lives to documenting volcanoes. This photo taken by Maurice shows Katia observing a fire fountain in a protective suit. The husband-and-wife team were killed during the eruption of Mount Unzen in Japan in 1991.

SPACED-OUT SUIT
This protective suit has a metal coating that reflects the intense heat of a volcanic eruption and leaves the scientist inside cool. But it also inhibits the wearer from feeling, hearing, or seeing what is going on. In a tight spot, the bulky suit may stop him or her from running away to safety.

VOLCANO BIOGRAPHY
The volcanologist's notebook is the history of a volcano, rather like a chapter out of its biography. The observer makes notes and sketches of all the big (and small) events during an eruption. The significance of some things may only become clear later.

HOT ROD
This metal rod is ideal for collecting red-hot lava. From relative safety at one end of the pole, the volcanologist dips the far end into the lava flow. He or she then twists it around, hooking up a blob of lava. This cools quickly once it is pulled out of the main flow.

Hard hat

Gloves made from the heat-resistant mineral asbestos

TOO HOT TO HANDLE
To collect warm samples and work close to red-hot lava, volcanologists wear asbestos gloves. Hard hats protect against small volcanic bombs (p.18).

TAPE MEASURE
A tape measure is handy for checking cracks in the ground, which may widen imperceptibly from day to day.

Binoculars

A CLOSER LOOK
Binoculars allow people to get closer to a volcano (in this case, Kilauea in Hawaii) without getting too close.

PATHFINDER
The ground of an erupting volcano is continually changing, as new lava hardens into rock and builds new landforms. The mining transit is a surveying tool that is very good for simple, rapid mapping. It has a compass and a level (to find verticals and horizontals). Small and light, it can be clipped to the volcanologist's belt.

Level

Compass

Rotating stage

MAPPING THE MOVING EARTH
A precise level can detect the small changes in ground level that foretell an eruption.

Folding, portable tripod

Thermometer reading up to 250°C

TAKING THE VOLCANO'S TEMPERATURE
Katia Krafft risks searing heat to take the temperature of a lava flow on Piton de la Fournaise volcano, Réunion (pp.22–23). She is not using a glass thermometer, which would melt, but a kind of electric thermometer called a thermocouple. The reading was 2,012°F (1,100°C), 540°F (300°C) less than the melting point of steel.

Volcanoes on other planets

SPACE EXPLORATION HAS SHOWN that volcanic activity is one of the most important geological processes in the solar system. The many space missions of the last two decades have brought back photographs and even rock samples. Some craft will never return to Earth, but continue to travel into deep space, beaming back information that can be translated by computers into detailed images of the more distant planets. We now know that many planetary bodies are scarred by enormous craters. But few of these are volcanic. Most are impact craters, the scars left by collisions with meteorites. Like Earth, the Moon, Venus, and Mars have solid surfaces that have been partly shaped by volcanic activity. The volcanoes on the Moon and Mars have been extinct for many millions of years. Scientists suspect that Venus's volcanoes may still be active. But of all the other planets in our solar system, only Io, one of Jupiter's 16 moons, shows volcanoes that are still active and erupting.

TIDYING UP THE PLANET
The hero of Antoine de Saint-Exupéry's children's story *The Little Prince* lives on a planet (Asteroid B–612) with two active volcanoes. Before setting out on a journey, he cleans them out to be sure they won't erupt and make trouble while he's away; he knows this could happen if their throats get blocked and they cannot breathe. He also cleans out his one extinct volcano, because, as he says, "One never knows!"

molten rock

lava flow

SURFACE OF IO
This colored infrared image shows the Tvashtar Catena volcanic region on the surface of Io, one of Jupiter's moons. The image was taken by NASA's *Galileo Orbiter* spacecraft and shows molten rock and a 37-mile- (60-km-) long lava flow, produced by a volcanic eruption.

OLYMPUS MONS
The extinct volcano Olympus Mons is 370 miles (600 km) across and rises 15 miles (25 km) above the surrounding plain. This makes it the highest point on Mars—and the largest volcano yet found in the universe, bigger than the entire Hawaiian island chain (pp. 22–23). Huge calderas (p.39) nest one inside each other at its summit.

Clouds of ice shroud the summit

Volcano Sif

Volcano Gula

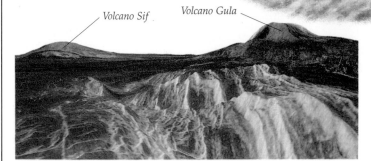

ERUPTING INTO SPACE
One of the most exciting discoveries in the exploration of the solar system was the erupting volcano Prometheus on Io. Seen in this *Voyager* image, the volcano is spewing a plume of gases 100 miles (160 km) above the solid surface. The plume looks pale against the black of space. The eruption clouds shoot far into space because Io has very low gravity and virtually no atmosphere.

BENEATH THE CLOUDS
The spacecraft *Magellan* used imaging radar to penetrate the dense atmosphere of Venus. The images revealed huge volcanoes and impact craters lurking beneath the clouds. Like most features on Venus, they were named after women, including goddesses from mythology.

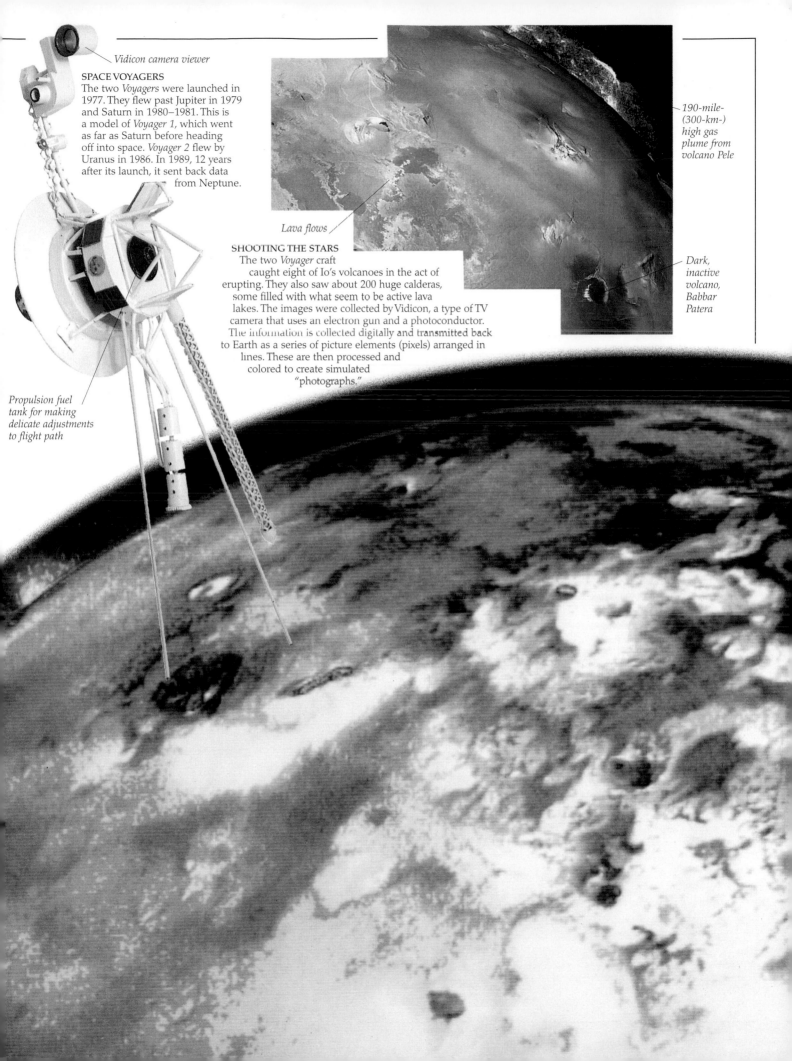

Vidicon camera viewer

SPACE VOYAGERS
The two *Voyagers* were launched in
1977. They flew past Jupiter in 1979
and Saturn in 1980–1981. This is
a model of *Voyager 1*, which went
as far as Saturn before heading
off into space. *Voyager 2* flew by
Uranus in 1986. In 1989, 12 years
after its launch, it sent back data
from Neptune.

*190-mile-
(300-km-)
high gas
plume from
volcano Pele*

Lava flows

SHOOTING THE STARS
The two *Voyager* craft
caught eight of Io's volcanoes in the act of
erupting. They also saw about 200 huge calderas,
some filled with what seem to be active lava
lakes. The images were collected by Vidicon, a type of TV
camera that uses an electron gun and a photoconductor.
The information is collected digitally and transmitted back
to Earth as a series of picture elements (pixels) arranged in
lines. These are then processed and
colored to create simulated
"photographs."

*Dark,
inactive
volcano,
Babbar
Patera*

*Propulsion fuel
tank for making
delicate adjustments
to flight path*

When the earth moves

Cartoon about the San Francisco quake of 1906, captioned "I hope I never have one of those splitting headaches again."

BEING IN A LARGE EARTHQUAKE is a terrifying experience. The shaking of the ground we stand on is profoundly disturbing, both physically and psychologically. When the shaking starts, there is no knowing how long it will go on or how severe it will be. Only when it stops is there some certainty in life again. The longest tremor ever recorded, the Alaskan earthquake of March 23, 1964, lasted four minutes (p.57). But most quakes last less than a minute. In those brief moments, homes, stores, even entire cities are destroyed. The earth sometimes seems to undulate. Afterward, great cracks may appear in the ground. Even stranger, the rocks may show no sign at all of the intense undulations they went through in the shaking. People also seem to find the many months of small earthquakes (aftershocks) that follow a big tremor very disturbing.

DISASTER MOVIE
This film about an earthquake destroying Los Angeles was shown in "Sensurround"—low-frequency sounds meant to simulate earthquake shaking.

SHAKEN TO THE FOUNDATIONS
Almost 75 years old, these wooden buildings in the Marina District of San Francisco were built on a landfill site. They slipped off their foundations as the filled land settled in the shaking of the 1989 earthquake (p.7).

PANIC SETS IN
People leave buildings and rush into the streets in panic as an earthquake shakes the city of Valparaíso, Chile, in 1906. Masonry buildings are collapsing as their walls crumble.

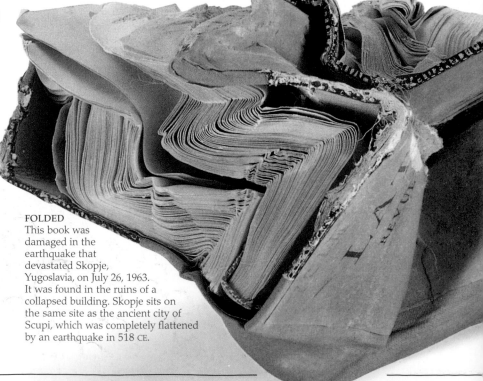

FOLDED
This book was damaged in the earthquake that devastated Skopje, Yugoslavia, on July 26, 1963. It was found in the ruins of a collapsed building. Skopje sits on the same site as the ancient city of Scupi, which was completely flattened by an earthquake in 518 CE.

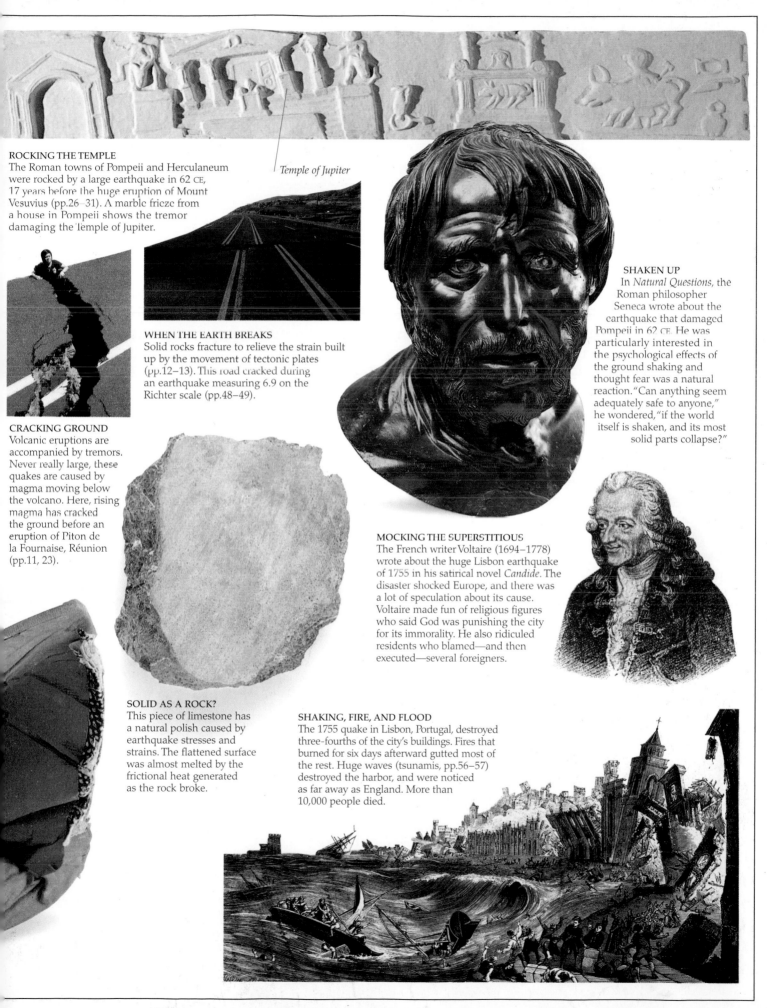

ROCKING THE TEMPLE
The Roman towns of Pompeii and Herculaneum were rocked by a large earthquake in 62 CE, 17 years before the huge eruption of Mount Vesuvius (pp.26–31). A marble frieze from a house in Pompeii shows the tremor damaging the Temple of Jupiter.

Temple of Jupiter

WHEN THE EARTH BREAKS
Solid rocks fracture to relieve the strain built up by the movement of tectonic plates (pp.12–13). This road cracked during an earthquake measuring 6.9 on the Richter scale (pp.48–49).

CRACKING GROUND
Volcanic eruptions are accompanied by tremors. Never really large, these quakes are caused by magma moving below the volcano. Here, rising magma has cracked the ground before an eruption of Piton de la Fournaise, Réunion (pp.11, 23).

SHAKEN UP
In *Natural Questions*, the Roman philosopher Seneca wrote about the earthquake that damaged Pompeii in 62 CE. He was particularly interested in the psychological effects of the ground shaking and thought fear was a natural reaction. "Can anything seem adequately safe to anyone," he wondered, "if the world itself is shaken, and its most solid parts collapse?"

MOCKING THE SUPERSTITIOUS
The French writer Voltaire (1694–1778) wrote about the huge Lisbon earthquake of 1755 in his satirical novel *Candide*. The disaster shocked Europe, and there was a lot of speculation about its cause. Voltaire made fun of religious figures who said God was punishing the city for its immorality. He also ridiculed residents who blamed—and then executed—several foreigners.

SOLID AS A ROCK?
This piece of limestone has a natural polish caused by earthquake stresses and strains. The flattened surface was almost melted by the frictional heat generated as the rock broke.

SHAKING, FIRE, AND FLOOD
The 1755 quake in Lisbon, Portugal, destroyed three-fourths of the city's buildings. Fires that burned for six days afterward gutted most of the rest. Huge waves (tsunamis, pp.56–57) destroyed the harbor, and were noticed as far away as England. More than 10,000 people died.

Intensity and magnitude

HOW DO YOU MEASURE THE SIZE of an earthquake? News reports usually give the quake a magnitude on the Richter scale. The Richter magnitude is useful because it can be worked out from a recording—called a seismogram—of the earthquake waves (pp.52–55). The waves of a big quake can be recorded on the other side of the globe. As as long as the distance between the recording device and the quake's center is taken into account, the Richter magnitude can be calculated from anywhere on the planet. But where the shaking is felt, it is more important to know how intense the shaking was and how it affected buildings and people. This is called the intensity of shaking. It is measured on a different scale, such as the modified Mercalli intensity scale. Intensity is purely descriptive and cannot be recorded by a machine. Instead, it is compiled by inspecting the damage and getting the quake's survivors to fill in questionnaires. Every earthquake has just one Richter magnitude. But because the damage it does falls off away from its center, it has many intensities, which also decrease away from the center.

Giuseppe
Mercalli
(1850–1914)

Intensity

The Italian volcanologist Giuseppe Mercalli created his intensity scale in 1902. He used 12 grades with Roman numerals from I to XII. His scale was later updated to create the modified Mercalli intensity scale.

I The shaking is not felt by people, but instruments record it.

II People at rest notice the shaking (above), especially if they are on the upper floors of buildings. Delicately suspended objects may swing.

III People indoors feel a vibration like the passing of a light truck. Hanging objects swing (above). Length of shaking can be estimated, but people may not recognize it as an earthquake.

IV Vibration like a heavy truck passing. Dishes rattle and wooden walls creak. Standing cars rock.

V Felt outdoors. Liquid in glasses slops out (above), small objects knocked over. Doors swing open and close.

VI Felt by all. Many are frightened and rush outdoors. People walk unsteadily; windows, dishes break (above). Pictures fall off walls; small bells ring.

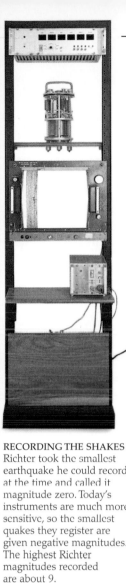

Magnitude

Working in California in the 1930s, Charles Richter wanted to compare the sizes of local earthquakes. He used the wiggly tracings of the shaking that are recorded on seismographs (pp.52–55). Knowing how far he was from each quake, he applied a distance factor to the maximum wiggle. After allowing for the characteristics of the instrument, he came up with the quake's magnitude. Richter's scale is used today all over the world.

American seismologist Charles F. Richter (1900–1985)

RECORDING THE SHAKES
Richter took the smallest earthquake he could record at the time and called it magnitude zero. Today's instruments are much more sensitive, so the smallest quakes they register are given negative magnitudes. The highest Richter magnitudes recorded are about 9.

Intensity contours for an earthquake that struck Japan on May 22, 1925

Epicenter

II III IV V VI

VII Difficult to stand (above). Furniture broken, plaster and loose bricks crack and fall. Waves on ponds. Large bells ring.

VIII Steering of cars affected. Damage to masonry walls, some of which fall. Falling chimneys, steeples (above), monuments. Branches off trees. Changes in flow of wells and springs. Cracks in wet ground.

IX General panic. Animals run in confusion. General damage to foundations of buildings. Frame buildings, if not bolted down, shifted off their foundations (above). Sand, mud, and water bubble out of ground.

X Most masonry and frame buildings destroyed with their foundations (above). Some well-built wooden buildings destroyed. Large landslides. Water thrown out of rivers and canals.

XI Railroad tracks greatly distorted. Underground pipelines completely out of service. Highways useless. Ground distorted by large cracks. Many large landslides and rock falls.

XII Practically all built structures above and below ground destroyed or useless (above). Ground surface much altered with cracks and slumps. River courses moved, waterfalls appear. Waves seen on ground surface.

Waves of destruction

Eartquake waves travel fast—about 16,000 mph (25,000 km/h) in rock, slower in soft sands and muds. In the seconds after the rock fracture that causes earthquake shaking, shock waves travel out in all directions. Usually they are most devastating near the epicenter, the spot on the surface nearest to where the rocks have fractured. But sometimes the waves are slowed down and concentrated by soft sands and muds. This can cause severe shaking even far from the epicenter. The first waves to arrive are primary or P waves. They are fastest because they travel like sound waves, with a push–pull movement that does not distort the rock they pass through very much. The slower secondary or S waves are the next to arrive. They travel at slightly more than half the speed, as they distort the rocks in a more complicated sideways-shearing movement. The slowest waves, surface waves, move in the most complex way. They only develop fully a long way from the epicenter.

SEISMOGRAM

This is a recording of a 5.1 Richter magnitude quake. The time lag between the P and S waves—in this case, 17 seconds—is used to calculate the distance from the focus. The magnitude is calculated from the maximum P-wave amplitude, taking into account the distance and the sensitivity of the seismograph.

P wave of maximum amplitude

Time scale

— 17 seconds —

First P wave   First S wave

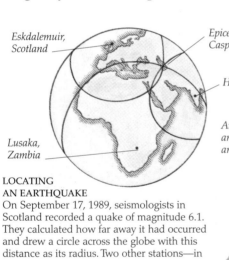

Eskdalemuir, Scotland

Epicenter in Caspian Sea

Hyderabad, India

Lusaka, Zambia

LOCATING AN EARTHQUAKE

On September 17, 1989, seismologists in Scotland recorded a quake of magnitude 6.1. They calculated how far away it had occurred and drew a circle across the globe with this distance as its radius. Two other stations—in Africa and India—made calculations and drew distance circles. They met in the Caspian Sea, the epicenter of the quake.

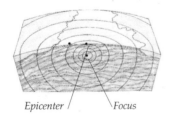

Epicenter   Focus

DEEP FOCUS

An earthquake's focus—the area where the rocks have fractured—is usually many miles inside Earth. On the surface, the waves are strongest at the epicenter, the point directly above the focus.

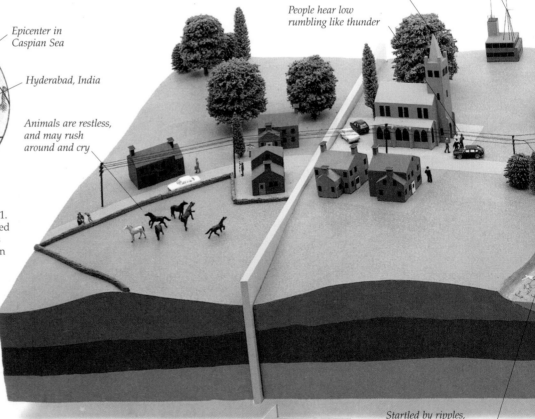

Seismic station records first P-waves

Church bells ring

People hear low rumbling like thunder

Animals are restless, and may rush around and cry

Startled by ripples, water birds fly off ponds

P waves

BEFORE THE EARTHQUAKE

Animals (and some people) may feel uncomfortable in the minutes before an earthquake strikes. They seem to sense that something is not quite right.

THE FIRST WAVES STRIKE

The first waves to arrive, P waves, may be so small that they are heard but not felt.

DEVASTATED IN A MINUTE
The town of Pointe-à-Pitre on the Caribbean island of Guadeloupe was shaken by an earthquake of Richter magnitude 8 on February 8, 1843. Eyewitnesses said the shaking lasted for about a minute. This was long enough to reduce most of the buildings to ruins. A fire that followed torched what was left of the town.

Woman sits by the ruins of her house in Lice, Turkey

Living through an earthquake

This model shows the waves of shaking from a large earthquake as they pass through the countryside. The epicenter is far off the page to the right. The fast P waves (in yellow) have gone the farthest and are about to strike the area on the far left. S waves (blue) follow, causing considerable damage. The slowest waves, surface waves (red), arrive seconds later. They have just reached the right of the model, where they have caused the total collapse of buildings already weakened by the S waves.

Trees and bushes shake and rustle

Ground cracks open

Cracks appear in buildings

Vehicles cannot follow straight lines

Sand and water bubble out of ground for hours after shaking stops

Fires start in ruins

Trees are uprooted

Landslide

People panic, have trouble standing up

Many buildings in ruins

S waves

Surface waves

SECONDARY WAVES STRIKE
The S waves follow the P waves. Here the waves are shaking and distorting buildings until they crack or even collapse.

SURFACE WAVES
Some quakes generate powerful surface waves. They can cause serious damage far from the epicenter.

Measuring earthquake waves

THE FIRST INSTRUMENT FOR RECORDING EARTHQUAKES was built by the Chinese scientist Zhang Heng in the second century CE. The original instrument did not survive and we only know of it from contemporary descriptions. It was a huge device about 6 ft (2 m) across and built of bronze. It could record earthquakes too slight to be noticed otherwise. The device could also tell roughly which direction the quake had come from. But because it gave no more information, we now call it a seismoscope. Not until 1856, soon after the discovery of electricity, was a more sophisticated earthquake recorder invented. Built by the Italian Luigi Palmieri, it is a seismograph, a device that writes a permanent trace—known as a seismogram— of the earthquake shaking. It was also set up to measure the overall size of the earthquake shaking (pp.48–49).

Inner workings of Zhang Heng's seismoscope

Pendulum

Suspension mechanism pulls on dragon's mouth

EARLY SEISMOLOGIST
The Chinese were keeping lists of earthquakes as early as 780 BCE. In the fourth century BCE, the Greek philosopher Aristotle suggested that tremors were caused by unstable vapors. But it was not until 132 CE that the Chinese geographer and astronomer Zhang Heng (78–139) invented the first seismoscope.

TOADS AND DRAGONS
Zhang Heng's seismoscope is a bronze vessel ringed with dragons and toads. A heavy pendulum hangs inside. During a tremor, the vessel moves more than the heavy pendulum. This triggers one or more dragons to open their jaws. Bronze balls held there are released, dropping into the open mouths of the toads that wait below.

Ball held in dragon's mouth

The toad that is farthest from the epicenter catches the falling ball. This indicates which direction the quake came from

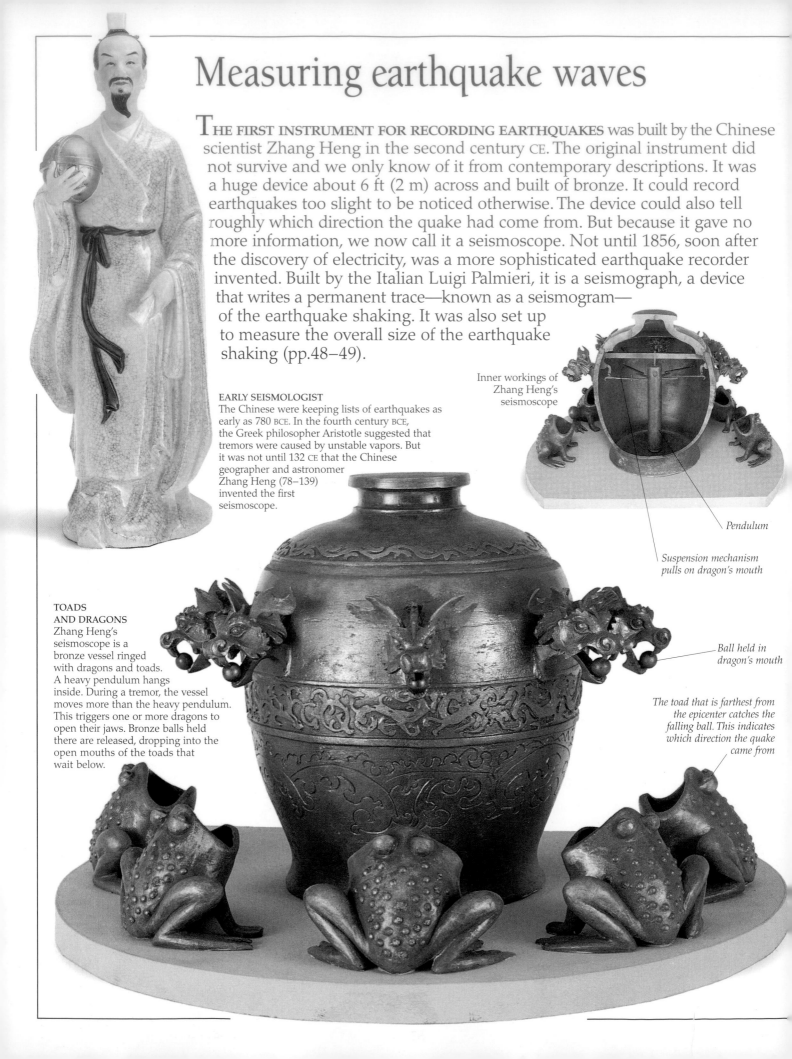

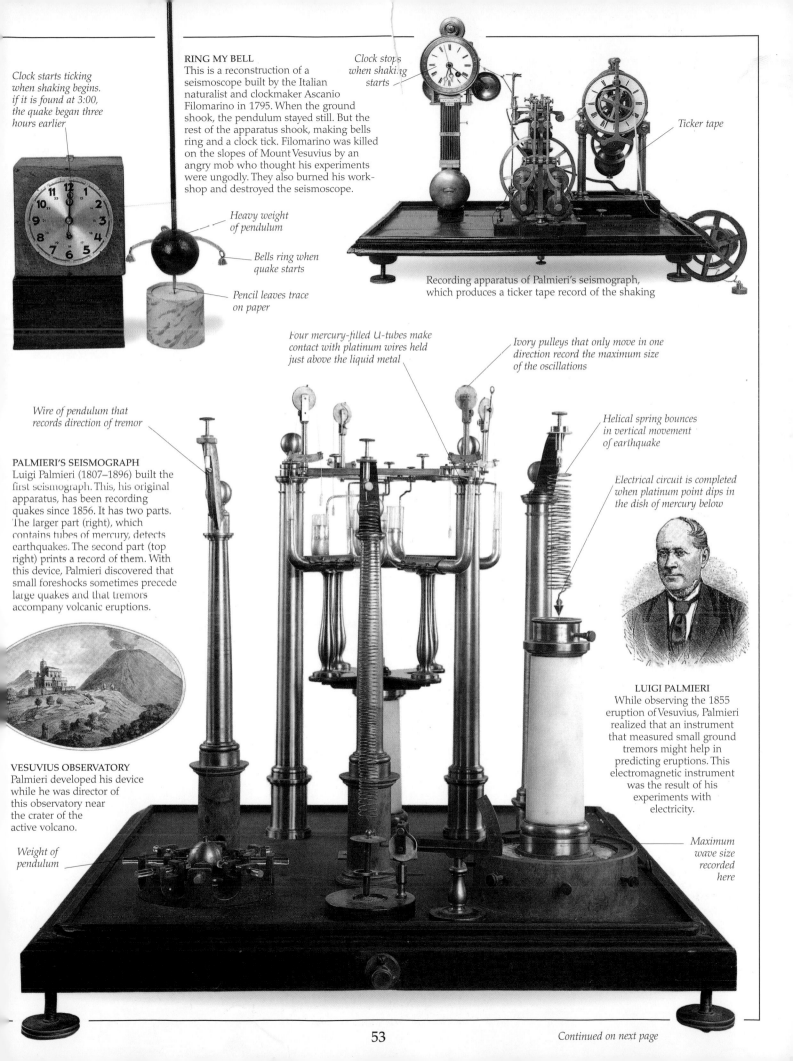

Clock starts ticking when shaking begins. if it is found at 3:00, the quake began three hours earlier

RING MY BELL
This is a reconstruction of a seismoscope built by the Italian naturalist and clockmaker Ascanio Filomarino in 1795. When the ground shook, the pendulum stayed still. But the rest of the apparatus shook, making bells ring and a clock tick. Filomarino was killed on the slopes of Mount Vesuvius by an angry mob who thought his experiments were ungodly. They also burned his workshop and destroyed the seismoscope.

Clock stops when shaking starts

Ticker tape

Heavy weight of pendulum

Bells ring when quake starts

Pencil leaves trace on paper

Recording apparatus of Palmieri's seismograph, which produces a ticker tape record of the shaking

Four mercury-filled U-tubes make contact with platinum wires held just above the liquid metal

Ivory pulleys that only move in one direction record the maximum size of the oscillations

Wire of pendulum that records direction of tremor

Helical spring bounces in vertical movement of earthquake

PALMIERI'S SEISMOGRAPH
Luigi Palmieri (1807–1896) built the first seismograph. This, his original apparatus, has been recording quakes since 1856. It has two parts. The larger part (right), which contains tubes of mercury, detects earthquakes. The second part (top right) prints a record of them. With this device, Palmieri discovered that small foreshocks sometimes precede large quakes and that tremors accompany volcanic eruptions.

Electrical circuit is completed when platinum point dips in the dish of mercury below

VESUVIUS OBSERVATORY
Palmieri developed his device while he was director of this observatory near the crater of the active volcano.

Weight of pendulum

LUIGI PALMIERI
While observing the 1855 eruption of Vesuvius, Palmieri realized that an instrument that measured small ground tremors might help in predicting eruptions. This electromagnetic instrument was the result of his experiments with electricity.

Maximum wave size recorded here

Continued on next page

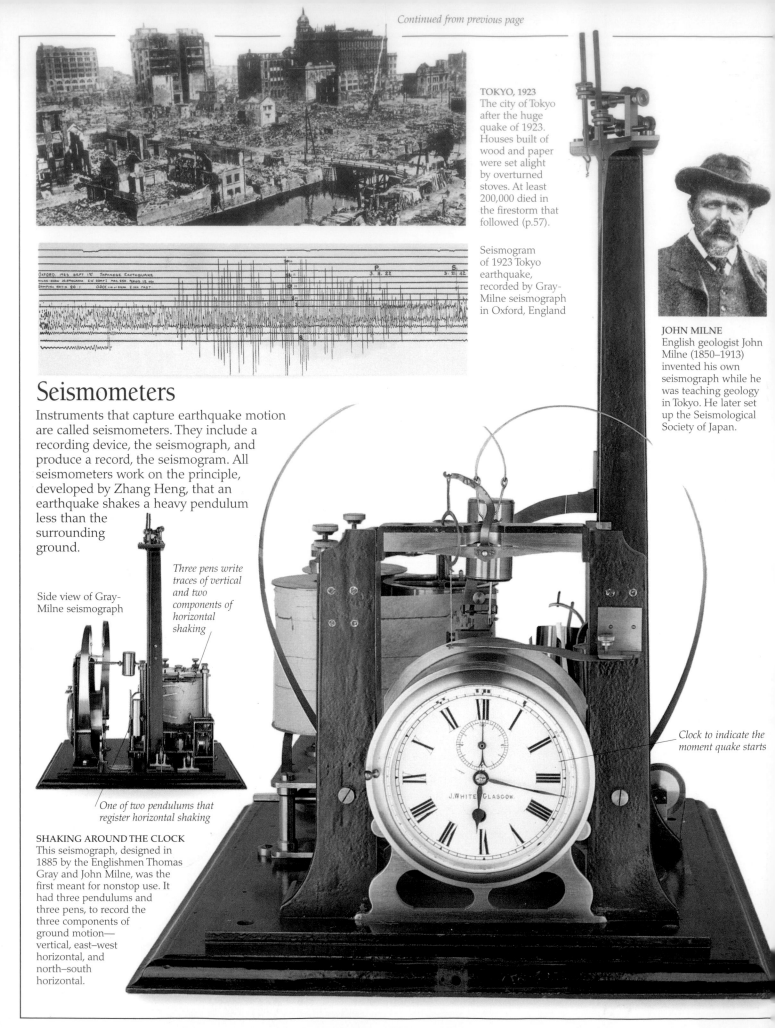

Continued from previous page

TOKYO, 1923
The city of Tokyo after the huge quake of 1923. Houses built of wood and paper were set alight by overturned stoves. At least 200,000 died in the firestorm that followed (p.57).

Seismogram of 1923 Tokyo earthquake, recorded by Gray-Milne seismograph in Oxford, England

OXFORD. 1923 SEPT 1ST JAPANESE EARTHQUAKE
MILNE-SHAW SEISMOGRAM EW COMP'T MAG 250 PERIOD 15 SEC
DAMPING RATIO 20:1 CLOCK 1/2 MIN OF SEISM. E SEC FAST

JOHN MILNE
English geologist John Milne (1850–1913) invented his own seismograph while he was teaching geology in Tokyo. He later set up the Seismological Society of Japan.

Seismometers

Instruments that capture earthquake motion are called seismometers. They include a recording device, the seismograph, and produce a record, the seismogram. All seismometers work on the principle, developed by Zhang Heng, that an earthquake shakes a heavy pendulum less than the surrounding ground.

Side view of Gray-Milne seismograph

Three pens write traces of vertical and two components of horizontal shaking

Clock to indicate the moment quake starts

One of two pendulums that register horizontal shaking

SHAKING AROUND THE CLOCK
This seismograph, designed in 1885 by the Englishmen Thomas Gray and John Milne, was the first meant for nonstop use. It had three pendulums and three pens, to record the three components of ground motion— vertical, east–west horizontal, and north–south horizontal.

A MODERN OBSERVATORY

At the Vesuvius Observatory, great reels of paper record the ground movement measured by a series of seismometers set up at strategic points in the area. Many modern earthquake stations place their seismometers in remote places or deep in boreholes. Here they are far from confusing signals like heavy car or air traffic or quarrying. Their data is beamed into the recording center by radio or along telephone lines. Modern seismographs record on magnetic tape, which allows for much better analysis.

PORTABLE

Networks of portable seismometers are used to monitor aftershocks of big quakes and ground tremors during volcanic eruptions. They were also used to prove that earthquakes did not cause the Lake Nyos disaster (p.20).

MOONQUAKES

American astronauts left seismometers on the Moon to record moonquakes. Many moonquakes are caused by meteorites hitting the surface. Others seem to take place most often when the Moon is closest to the Earth.

Case hides inverted, suspended pendulum

Paper drum winds very slowly between earthquakes. When shaking starts, gears change and the drum starts feeding the paper through much faster

Handle for winding up weight that turns drum

Damping system, which makes sure that each shock wave is only recorded once

Suspended weight drives paper drum (mechanical clocks driven in same way)

Smoked paper seismogram

Arm from which pendulums are suspended

SMOKING UP

Early seismographs, many still in use, scratch their traces on smoked paper. This avoids the problems of ink, which can run out or gum up—a disaster during tremors. The paper is smoked by coating it in the carbon produced by burning oil.

HEAVY DUTY

This is a restored version of the seismograph invented by the German Emil Wiechert (1861–1928) in 1908. Its 440-lb (200-kg) mass measures the two horizontal components of ground shaking. It worked in tandem with a smaller instrument that measured vertical motion. Here, an inverted pendulum consists of a stiff rod balanced on a movable base that is very sensitive to any horizontal motion. An even bigger Wiechert instrument has been operating in Uppsala, Sweden, since 1904.

Mud, flood, and avalanche

THE TRAUMA OF AN EARTHQUAKE or volcanic eruption may have devastating repercussions. Large ash eruptions are often followed by landslides or mud flows. The ash that piles up near the crater may collapse, bringing part of the mountain down with it. Heavy rain often adds to the problem, creating a wet slurry that turns into a mud flow. In mountains, both quakes and eruptions may trigger avalanches; by or beneath the sea, they can both cause giant water waves. These are popularly known as "tidal waves." But as they are not created by tides, scientists prefer the Japanese name, *tsunami*. Tsunamis may travel across oceans. When they break on faraway shores, the great walls of water can wreak horrendous damage.

SWEPT AWAY
The ashy eruptions of Mount Pinatubo in the Philippines (p.17) were accompanied by mud flows that swept away roads, bridges, and several villages. The flows were caused by torrential rain falling on newly erupted ash.

Overview of Armero mud flow, 1985

BURIED IN A SEA OF MUD
In November 1985, an eruption of Ruiz Volcano in Colombia, South America spewed clouds of ash and pumice onto the snow and ice fields of the mountain's summit. This melted part of the snow, which in turn wet the ash, turning it into a moving slurry. The heavy mud flow cascaded down the Lagunillas Canyon at speeds up to 20 mph (35 km/h). The city of Armero, 36 miles (60 km) away at the mouth of the canyon, was devastated by the roaring torrent of mud (left and below). Some 22,000 people were buried alive by the waves of mud, rock, and debris that set around them like wet concrete. The only survivors were rescued from the edge of the flow (p.58).

Truck trapped in mud, Armero

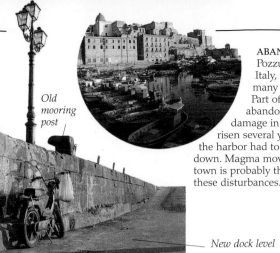

ABANDONED TOWN
Pozzuoli, near Naples, Italy, has been shaken by many small earthquakes. Part of the town was abandoned after shaking damage in 1983. The town has risen several yards since then, so the harbor had to be rebuilt lower down. Magma moving below the town is probably the cause of all these disturbances.

Old mooring post

New dock level

DWARFING FUJI
Japanese coastlines are plagued by tsunamis from both volcanic eruptions and earthquakes. The volcano Fujiyama (p.6) can be seen in the background of *Giant Wave*, a picture of a tsunami by Katsushika Hokusai (1760–1849).

TSUNAMI
In December 2004, movement along a submarine fault deep below the seabed of the eastern Indian Ocean generated a series of catastrophic tsunamis that spread out across the Indian Ocean. Coastal communities as far away as Sri Lanka and Africa suffered death and destruction, but the highest death tolls were experienced in the islands of southeast Asia—in the village of Calang on Sumatra, only 1,000 of a population of 5,000 survived.

KRAKATAU, WEST OF JAVA
Tsunamis as high as 100 ft (30 m) crashed into surrounding islands after the cataclysmic eruption of Krakatoa (now called Krakatau, p.35). The walls of water flattened many villages on Sumatra and Java (which is actually east of Krakatau), killing 36,000 people.

AVALANCHE
Earthquake shaking may trigger avalanches that were just waiting to happen. In 1970, a magnitude 7.7 quake off the coast of Peru caused a disastrous slide of snow and rock that fell 13,200 ft (4,000 m) and killed over 50,000 people in the valley below.

FIRE IN THE RUINS
Firefighters douse a blaze after the 1989 San Francisco earthquake (p.7). The fires that follow quakes or eruptions can raze cities. If gas lines are broken or inflammable liquids spilled, the slightest spark causes fire. Shaking often damages the underground water supply, making a blaze harder to fight. The large 1923 Tokyo quake (p.54) was followed by a terrifying firestorm that swept through the city's wooden houses and left 200,000 dead.

State of emergency

THE CHAOS THAT FOLLOWS a big earthquake or volcanic eruption makes rescue difficult and dangerous. Many people may be killed by collapsing buildings in the few seconds that violent earthquake shaking lasts. More die from injuries in the next few hours. But people trapped in fallen masonry may survive for days. For rescuers, finding them and getting them out is a race against time. It may be hard to rescue trapped people without putting more people at risk. Half-collapsed buildings may topple further at any moment. Hazardous substances could suddenly catch fire or explode. In ash-flow or mud-flow eruptions, no one knows when to expect another surge or flow. Damage to telephone lines, television and radio links, and electricity, gas, and water supplies makes rescue operations even harder to mount.

PERILOUS RESCUE
A survivor is lifted by helicopter from the setting mud in Armero, Colombia in 1985 (p.56).

MUDDY ESCAPE
An unconscious survivor is rescued from the mud flows that engulfed Armero in 1985. Some 36 miles (60 km) from the volcano, parts of the mud flow were still hot, and survivors had to be treated for burns.

Controls showing level of infrared radiation

FINDING LIVE BODIES
A thermal image camera is used to locate people trapped after an earthquake. Survivors are often buried, wounded or unconscious, in the rubble of their collapsed homes. The camera uses infrared radiation to detect the heat of a living person. The problem is distinguishing the heat of a body from the natural heat of other objects. This is easiest early in the morning, when the background heat is lowest.

Strap worn around neck ensures that expensive camera is not dropped in rubble

HAVE CAMERA, WILL TRAVEL
The London Fire and Civil Defence Authority uses thermal image cameras to find survivors after all kinds of disasters. It sends trained teams to disaster zones, like northwest Iran after the massive quake of June 1990.

Searcher wears headphones to listen for human sounds in the wreckage

Italian newspaper illustration from 1906 showing a boy being rescued from the remains of his home after an earthquake

TRAPPED PERSON DETECTOR
This device was used after the Armenian earthquake of 1988. Thousands of people were buried when multi-story buildings collapsed in heaps of rubble. Some were successfully located with this detector, which works by detecting vibrations.

Microphone, so rescuer can talk to trapped person

Red two-way electrode allows rescuer to converse with survivor

Yellow one-way electrode picks up vibrations

SENSITIVE NOSE
Alongside technological equipment, sniffer dogs play their part in the race to find survivors after an earthquake. The aftershocks that usually follow the main quake are a big hazard. Rescuers are often at risk as they work in the precarious remains of buildings. If an aftershock causes further collapse, the rescuers may have to be rescued, too.

KASHMIR EARTHQUAKE
Some 38,000 people were killed in Pakistan in October 2005, when a magnitude 7.6 earthquake hit Kashmir. Many hill villages such as Balakot were almost completely destroyed.

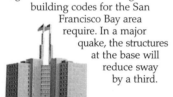

Italian magazines produced for the 1990s, the International Decade for Natural Disaster Reduction

Preparing for disaster

EARTHQUAKES AND VOLCANIC ERUPTIONS are natural events that have been happening throughout Earth's history. As the planet's population increases, more and more people are living in danger zones, along faults or close to active volcanoes. When one of these natural events upsets human life, many people may die and their buildings and farmland may be destroyed. In the aftermath, disease and famine may be even more destructive. We cannot hope to stop disasters entirely. But as knowledge of Earth's workings increases, wise planning can reduce their number and scale. Learning to live in disaster zones means actively monitoring volcanoes and fault lines and building cities that can withstand earthquake shaking. It also means education, so people know what to do in an emergency.

BUILDING CITIES THAT WON'T FALL DOWN

Many modern cities are in earthquake-prone regions. One way to reduce disaster is to design buildings that can withstand the deadly shaking. The Transamerica Pyramid looks precarious, but it is designed to be twice as strong as building codes for the San Francisco Bay area require. In a major quake, the structures at the base will reduce sway by a third.

LIVING IN THE SHADOW
Two thousand years after the volcano's greatest eruption, over two million people now live in the Bay of Naples in the shadow of Mount Vesuvius. This is modern Herculaneum, a thriving town that surrounds the ruins of Roman Herculaneum.

FRANK LLOYD WRIGHT
This American architect was a pioneer in the design of earthquake-resistant buildings. His Imperial Hotel in Tokyo survived the 1923 quake almost unscathed.

SHAKE TILL THEY DROP
Built in 1923, this pioneering Japanese shaking table was used to test models of buildings to see how they stood up to severe shaking. Modern shake tables are controlled by computers.

MOST MEASURED PLACE

The town of Parkfield in central California straddles the San Andreas fault system. Seismologists have predicted a major earthquake here. A laser measuring system is being used to detect movements along the fault. The laser, mounted on a hilltop in Parkfield, bounces light off a network of detectors a few miles away on the other side of the fault. It can detect ground movement of less than a millimeter over six kilometers (3.7 miles).

MEASURING CREEP

A technician for the US Geological Survey emerges from a creepmeter. He has been measuring creep, slow movement along the fault. Creep releases stress along the fault without detectable shaking.

LEARNING FROM PAST DISASTERS

Earthquakes of the same size tend to happen in the same place at regular intervals. Studying large quakes—in this case, the one that rocked Pompeii in 62 CE (p.47)—may help scientists to predict the next big tremor.

FALLING MASONRY

In this earthquake drill, rescue workers are treating actors "hit" by falling masonry. Many were injured by falling brick and stone in the 1989 San Francisco earthquake. Designing buildings without heavy architectural ornaments or chimneys might cut down on casualties like these.

Earthquake rescue practice in Japan

EARTHQUAKE DRILL

In Japan and California, earthquake drills are a part of everyday life. Children learn to keep a flashlight and sturdy shoes by their beds, so they can get to safety even if a quake strikes at night. Many people rush outdoors, only to be hit by falling chimneys, roof tiles, or glass. The safest place indoors is under a solid piece of furniture like a table or beneath the frame of an archway or doorway.

Anger of the gods

AS LONG AS PEOPLE HAVE LIVED on Earth, they have been curious about natural events like earthquakes and volcanic eruptions. Myths are a way of recording or explaining these strange, often fantastic happenings. In many parts of the world, myths and legends handed down from generation to generation are the only history. Often these myths are not written down or have been put on the page only recently. Through the poetic language and spiritual ideas, it is sometimes possible to recognize real places or happenings. Most societies explain natural events as the workings of a god or gods. In this way they give the planet the kinds of emotions we expect from human beings. When the gods are angry, they may punish people with the fire of an eruption or the horrible shaking of an earthquake. People often react to such disasters by offering sacrifices or gifts to calm the gods. Societies near active volcanoes may see the fiery mountains as the workshops of the gods (p.36). Many gods are believed to live on the eerie summits of volcanoes, which are often shrouded in fire and cloud.

Christians in Naples, Italy, try to stop the 1906 eruption of Mount Vesuvius (p.31) with crosses and prayers

HUMAN SACRIFICE
In Nicaragua, people once threw their most beautiful young women into the lava lake at Masaya to stop the volcano from erupting.

Lava lake

POPOCATÉPETL
This Aztec illustration shows Popocatépetl, Mexico, one of the highest peaks in the Americas at 17,887 ft (5,452 m). Its name is Aztec for "smoking mountain." When the volcano erupted violently in the 1520s, the Aztecs believed the gods were angry at the Spanish *conquistadores* (conquerors) who had looted their temples.

RESPONSIBLE FROG
Many cultures believed that the ground they stood on was held up by some huge creature. The ancient Greeks and Romans thought the superhuman Atlas was carrying the weight (p.10). Mongolians believed in a gigantic frog. Each time the animal stumbled under his great burden, the ground shook with an earthquake. A similar Hindu myth says that Earth sits on the backs of eight giant elephants.

ONE-EYED GIANT
This is an aerial view of Mount Vesuvius. From above, such craters resemble giant eyes. They may have inspired the Greek myth of the Cyclops, a tribe of one-eyed giants who helped the fire god Hephaistos in his forge (below and p.36). Like craters, the Cyclops hurled fire and rocks when they were angry.

Destruction of Sodom and Gomorrah, by an unknown Flemish painter

SHAKING THE SEA FLOOR
When the Greek sea god Poseidon (known as Neptune to the Romans) was angry, he banged the sea floor with his trident. This created earthquakes and tsunamis (pp.56-57).

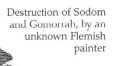

SODOM AND GOMORRAH
According to the Bible, God destroyed these cities with flood and fire because he was angry at their evil inhabitants. They may really have been devastated by some natural geological disaster.

Bronze figure of Hephaistos, first or second century BCE.

MASTER OF FIRE
The ancient Greeks believed the god Hephaistos had his fiery workshops under volcanoes (p.36). Another god, Prometheus, stole some of the fire from the volcanoes and gave it to mortals—a way of explaining how people discovered fire.

WHEN THE GODS ARE AWAY...
A Japanese myth says earthquakes are caused by the writhings of a giant catfish. Normally the gods keep the rascal under control by pinning it down with a large rock. But during October, when the gods are away, the fish may get loose. This wood-block print shows the gods flying back over the ruins of Edo (now Tokyo) after a big quake in October 1855. The leader of the gods is carrying the rock.

HOME OF THE GODS
Mount Fuji is thought to be the home of the god Kunitokotache (p.6). Fujiyama, the sacred spirit of the mountain, is said to protect the Japanese people. Legend says that the mountain can only be climbed by the pure of spirit. Many thousands make the ascent to the summit each year.

Did you know?

FASCINATING FACTS

Much of New Zealand's North Island, some 7,722 sq mi (20,000 sq km), and all island life, were devastated by vast pyroclastic flows from the eruption of the Lake Taupo caldera in 180 CE. Luckily, the first human inhabitants did not occupy the island until 1000 CE.

Around 200 black bears were killed in the eruption of Mount St. Helens

The effects of a volcano can be disastrous for wildlife. Figures from Mount St. Helens estimate that 11,000 hares, 6,000 deer, 5,200 elk, 1,400 coyotes, 300 bobcats, 200 black bears, and 15 mountain lions were killed by the blast.

The burning clouds of pyroclastic flows can travel at terrifying speeds of up to 300 mph (500 km/h) and reach temperatures of 1,470°F (800°C), burning everything in their path.

A truck flees from the burning clouds of Pinatubo, Philippines, 1991

At Pinatubo, pyroclastic flows traveling at over 40 mph (70 km/h) were recorded.

Where cracks form in the ocean floor as tectonic plates move apart, the water heated by the magma can reach temperatures of 1,224°F (662°C).

One of Iceland's greatest attractions used to be the Great Geyser, near Reykjavik, which had a jet 200–270 ft (60–80 m) high. When the geyser stopped spouting in 1916, people managed to reactivate it a few times using soap powder, but it is now just an 60-ft (18-m) hole.

In 1883, when Krakatau, in Indonesia, erupted, the noise was so powerful it burst the eardrums of sailors over 25 miles (40 km) away. Around 36,000 people died, most killed by the tsunamis— some 100 ft (30 m) tall—that devastated Java and Sumatra. Villages, ships, and boats were swept inland, including a large steamer, which was found 1.5 miles (2.6 km) inland.

Fires are a major problem after an earthquake. Fractured gas pipes mean fires spread rapidly and burst water mains dry up the hoses. This, together with streets blocked with debris, make the firefighters' work nearly impossible.

The greatest volcanic eruption in modern times was Tambora, Indonesia, in 1815. It produced 19.2 mi^3 (80 km^3) of volcanic ash, compared with just 0.24 mi^3 (1 km^3) measured at Mount St. Helens. In the last 10,000 years, only four eruptions have been as violent as Tambora.

In the open ocean, a tsunami can travel at incredible speeds of up to 370 mph (600 km/h).

A steamer swept inland after Krakatau erupted

Animals often show strange behavior before an earthquake. In 1975 in China, scientists successfully predicted an earthquake when they noticed snakes waking up from hibernation and rats swarming.

QUESTIONS AND ANSWERS

Q When is a volcano said to be extinct rather than dormant?

A Scientists put volcanoes into three categories. A volcano is classified as active if it has erupted within the last few hundred years. It is dormant if it has not erupted in the last few hundred years but has erupted during the last several thousand years. If a volcano has not erupted during the last several thousand years, it is said to be extinct.

Q Are earthquakes high on the Richter scale the most destructive?

A Not necessarily—all sorts of factors influence the effects of a quake, the geology of the rock in particular. Increasingly, earthquakes are measured on a scale called moment magnitude. This combines Richter readings with observations of rock movement to give a more accurate scale of destruction.

Q How many active volcanoes are there in the world?

A There are more than 1,500 active volcanoes in the world that rise above sea level. On average, each month around 20–30 are actually erupting. Some of these are volcanoes that erupt continually, like the Hawaiian volcanoes of Mauna Loa and Kilauea.

Earthquake drill at a school in the US

Q What should you do if there is an earthquake?

A At home, shelter in a doorway or under a strong table. In a public place, such as a classroom, find cover under a table or desk and protect your head with your arms. When the tremors stop, leave the building, and shelter as far as possible from walls, which may be unstable.

Q Have people ever tried to stop advancing lava flow?

A When the volcano on the Icelandic island of Heimaey erupted in 1973, the people tried to save the harbor on which the island depended from the lava. They did not stop it, but by spraying 6 million tons of sea water at the lava, they slowed it down and slightly altered its course. The lava flow stopped just 450 ft (137 m) from the harbor.

Mauna Loa, Hawaii

Q Could lava just come out of a crack in the earth?

A Yes; in 1943, in Parícutin, Mexico, a farmer found lava pouring from a crack that suddenly appeared in his field. Within a day there was a cone 33 ft (10 m) high. With eruptions over the following months, Parícutin grew layer by layer. After one year the lava was 1,476 ft (450 m) tall and had engulfed the nearby town.

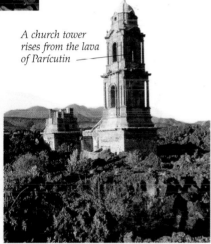
A church tower rises from the lava of Parícutin —
A town buried by lava, Parícutin, Mexico

Record Breakers

BIGGEST VOLCANO
Mauna Kea in Hawaii is a massive volcano, 4,446 ft (1,355 m) taller than Mount Everest, but because it rises out of the seabed, much of it is covered by sea water.

TALLEST GEYSER
The world's tallest geyser is the Steamboat Geyser in Yellowstone Park, Wyoming, with spray up to 195–380 ft (60–115 m). But in 1904, Waimangu Geyser, New Zealand, reached a height of 1,500 ft (460 m).

BIGGEST EARTHQUAKE
In 1960 an earthquake with a magnitude of 9.5 on the Richter scale was recorded in Chile. It caused tsunamis that reached Japan.

MOST DEVASTATING EARTHQUAKE
In 1556 an earthquake of 8.3 on the Richter scale killed 800,000 people in Shansi, China.

HIGHEST TSUNAMI WAVE
The highest tsunami wave recorded struck Ishigaki in Japan in 1971. The monstrous wave was 280 ft (85 m) high.

Timeline

OUR PLANET HAS A VIOLENT HISTORY and its constant activity continues to remind us that we live at the mercy of the natural world. The timeline below includes just some of the major volcanic eruptions and earthquakes of the past four thousand years. We have most information about events in living memory or from records in recent history, but volcanologists can look much farther back in time by studying the features of Earth's surface. It is thought that one of the biggest eruptions ever happened two million years ago in Yellowstone, Wyoming and was 250 times more powerful than that of Pinatubo in 1991.

Gas, dust, and rock explode from Mount St. Helens, 1980

ca. 1620 BCE SANTORINI, GREECE
Violent eruptions blew the island of Santorini apart and buried it under 100 ft (30 m) of pumice.

79 CE VESUVIUS, ITALY
A burning cloud of volcanic ash engulfed the Roman towns of Pompeii and Herculaneum, killing thousands.

1755 LISBON, PORTUGAL
A powerful earthquake measuring 8.5 on the Richter scale shook Portugal's capital, reducing it to rubble.

1783 SKAFTAR FIRES, ICELAND
A fissure (crack) 16 miles (27 km) long opened up in the Earth's surface, spewing out poisonous gases and red-hot lava.

Craters mark Skaftar fissure today

1815 TAMBORA, INDONESIA
The biggest eruption ever recorded. Around 90,000 Indonesians were killed. It is believed that the dust ejected reduced levels of sunlight around the world and affected the climate of the planet dramatically.

1883 KRAKATAU, INDONESIA
The enormous force of Krakatau's eruption left a crater 960 ft (290 m) deep in the ocean floor and created huge tsunamis that devastated the coastlines of Java and Sumatra.

1902 MOUNT PELÉE, MARTINIQUE
All but two of the entire population of Saint-Pierre were wiped out by the burning cloud of gas and dust that raced down the sides of Mount Pelée at speeds of 100 mph (160 km/h). Around 30,000 people died.

A watch stopped by the eruption of Mount Pelée, 1902

1906 SAN FRANCISCO, CA
Two huge earth tremors hit the city, setting off fires that burned for many days. The earthquake is estimated to have measured 8.3 on the Richter scale.

1920 XINING, CHINA
The entire province of Gansu was devastated when shaken by an earthquake measuring 8.6 on the Richter scale. Over 180,000 people were killed.

1923 TOKYO, JAPAN
An earthquake of 8.3 on the Richter scale flattened 600,000 homes and knocked over stoves, which started a terrible firestorm.

1943 PARÍCUTIN, MEXICO
Lava began to flow from a crack that appeared in a farmer's field. By 1952 the cone stood 1,732 ft (528 m) tall.

1963 SURTSEY, ICELAND
Undersea volcanic explosions created a new island off the southwest coast of Iceland.

1963 SKOPJE, MACEDONIA
A violent earthquake destroyed more than 15,000 homes, leaving three-quarters of the town of Skopje homeless. At least 1,000 people were killed.

The ruins of San Francisco, 1906

Cinders engulf Vestmannaeyjar, Iceland

1973 HEIMAEY, ICELAND
Eldfell volcano erupted after 5,000 years of dormancy. Molten lava engulfed one-third of the town of Vestmannaeyjar on the Icelandic island of Heimaey.

1976 TANGSHAN, CHINA
The most disastrous earthquake in modern times. A massive tremor of 8.3 on the Richter scale almost completely destroyed the city of Tangshan and killed over 240,000 people.

1980 MOUNT ST. HELENS, WA
The eruption of Mount St. Helens sent gas, ash, and rock hurtling down the mountain, devastating vast areas around the volcano.

1985 MEXICO CITY, MEXICO
Powerful earth tremors, measuring 8.1 on the Richter scale, shook Mexico City for three minutes. High-rise buildings in the city center crashed to the ground. One million people were left homeless.

1985 NEVADO DEL RUIZ, COLOMBIA
The eruption of the Ruiz volcano caused a massive mudflow that engulfed the town of Armero 36 miles (60 km) away and buried 22,000 people in the mud.

1988 SPITAK, ARMENIA
Armenia and northeastern Turkey were shaken by a powerful earth tremor that almost completely destroyed the town of Spitak and killed most of the population.

1991 KILAUEA, HAWAII
Kilauea volcano, gently active since 1983, suddenly produced large quantities of lava that buried 8 miles (13 km) of road, 181 homes, and a visitors' center.

1991 PINATUBO, PHILIPPINES
The most violent volcanic eruption of the twentieth century. Falling ash destroyed 42,000 homes and smothered land. Volcanic ash in the atmosphere lowered temperatures around the world.

1994 LOS ANGELES, CA
An earthquake under the city destroyed nine highways and 11,000 buildings in 30 seconds.

1995 KOBE, JAPAN
Kobe was badly damaged by the most powerful earthquake to hit a modern city, measuring 7.2 on the Richter scale. Buildings were also damaged in Kyoto, 40 miles (60 km) away.

1996 GRIMSVOTN, ICELAND
A 2.5-mile- (4-km-) long fissure appeared in the side of the Grimsvotn volcano, which lies below the Vatnajökull glacier in Iceland. Lava melting the glacier ice caused terrible flooding, which damaged roads, pipelines, and power cables.

1997 MONTSERRAT, ANTILLES
A series of major eruptions left two-thirds of the island of Montserrat uninhabitable, forcing 8,000 people to leave.

1998 NEW GUINEA
A violent offshore earthquake caused a 33-ft (10-m) high tsunami, which swept 1.2 miles (2 km) inland. Around 4,500 people died.

The destruction of the expressway, Kobe, Japan

2002 DEMOCRATIC REPUBLIC OF CONGO
About half a million people were forced to leave their homes when rivers of lava flowed from Mount Nyiragongo. The lava took a blazing path through Goma, destroying two-fifths of the town.

2004 SUMATRA-ANDAMAN, INDIAN OCEAN
An undersea earthquake, with an epicenter just off the west coast of Sumatra, Indonesia, triggered a series of tsunamis, killing around 187,000 people.

2005 PAKISTAN
Also known as the Kashmir earthquake, this violent quake, measuring 7.6 on the Richter scale, killed around 73,000 people and left 33 million homeless.

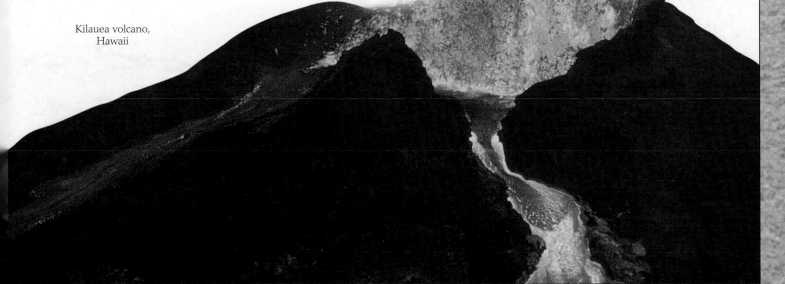

Kilauea volcano, Hawaii

Find out more

VOLCANOES ARE EXTREMELY UNPREDICTABLE and even experienced volcanologists have been killed in eruptions. However, there are volcanic national parks all over the world where you can see volcanic features safely, at first hand. There are also more accessible ways to find out about volcanoes, including sites on the Internet where you can find news of the latest eruptions and even watch volcanic activity live.

YELLOWSTONE PARK
A line of people can be seen here walking through the lunar-like landscape of the Norris geyser basin in Yellowstone National Park, Wyoming. Yellowstone lies on a volcanic hot spot and has a dramatic landscape with volcanic features such as geysers and fumaroles. It also experiences earthquakes. The park's most famous feature is the geyser named "Old Faithful."

THE STORY OF AN ERUPTION
The remains of the ancient cities of Pompeii and Herculaneum, near Naples, Italy (see pages 26–32), have not only taught scientists a lot about volcanoes but also give visitors invaluable insight into both volcanoes and life in ancient Roman times. Both cities were destroyed when Vesuvius erupted in 79 CE, but the mountain is still an active volcano—it last erupted in 1944. Weather permitting, visitors can climb up and look into the crater of the volcano.

The bodies of ancient Romans suffocated by the poisonous gases were preserved in the volcanic ash

The ruins of Pompeii lying in the shadow of Vesuvius

Places to visit

HAWAII VOLCANOES NATIONAL PARK
Explore Kilauea by car, or hike the park trails. If conditions are right, active lava flows may be observed from Chain of Craters Road.

MOUNT ST. HELENS NATIONAL MONUMENT
Explore areas devastated by the 1980 eruption, walk inside an ancient lava tube, and see the steaming lava dome inside the volcano crater.

ETNA, VESUVIUS, AND STROMBOLI, ITALY
The best-known of the Italian volcanoes are Etna in Sicily, the island of Stromboli, and Vesuvius near Naples. All can be climbed with guides, weather and volcanic activity permitting.

ICELAND
Iceland is still being formed by volcanic activity and has over two dozen volcanoes, but is most famous for its geysers and hot springs.

Runny pahoehoe lava flowing over a cliff made up of layer upon layer of lava

VISITING VOLCANOES
There are national parks worldwide where visitors can see signs of volcanic activity, past and present. Some of the best known are in Hawaii, the mainland US, Iceland, New Zealand, Japan, Mexico, and the Canary Islands. In Hawaii, there is almost constant volcanic activity. Visitors can drive to the rim of the active volcano, Kilauea, walk through a lava tube, and see an eruption from a safe distance.

Lava flow from Kilauea volcano in Hawaii

WATCHING THE EARTH

BECAUSE OF THE DANGERS, only trained volcanologists can monitor volcanoes closely, but on the Internet you can follow much of the work that such experts are doing all over the world. In the box below you will find the addresses of some websites with general background information on volcanology and links to lots of specific volcanoes. Some sites even have "volcanocams" so that you can watch volcanoes live, or almost live, online. For the most up-to-date information, the Smithsonian Institution produces an online weekly report on volcanic activity worldwide.

LIVING WITH A VOLCANO
These children are learning about Sakurajima Volcano in Japan. It is one of the most active volcanoes in the world, erupting around 150 times a year. Like many other active volcanoes, Sakurajima is monitored by a volcano observatory that collects data for research and to help predict activity that might endanger people's lives. Most observatories have websites with the latest information and pictures.

WATCHING FROM SPACE
This picture was taken by a Space Shuttle and shows thick clouds of ash and dust from the eruption of Kliuchevskoi Volcano in Russia in 1994. Volcanic ash clouds can cause pollution and affect climate and aviation. They are watched and measured by satellites. Amazing views of volcanoes on Earth and in space can be found on several websites.

DANGEROUS WORK
This volcanologist is checking gas samples inside the crater of Mount Erebus, Antarctica. It is dangerous work and in recent decades several volcanologists have been killed by unexpected eruptions. But this is just a small part of a volcanologist's work. Much more time is spent analyzing the data and advising people on the risks associated with volcanoes. There are many sites on the Internet where you can learn more about a volcanologist's work and find out how to become one.

USEFUL WEBSITES

- An introduction to volcanoes by Michigan Technical University: **www.geo.mtu.edu/volcanoes**
- Worldwide volcanic reference map: **www.geo.mtu.edu/volcanoes/world.html**
- Smithsonian Institution report on volcanic activity: **www.volcano.si.edu**
- US Geological Survey homepage with links to volcanoes: **www.usgs.gov**
- NASA directory of links to natural hazards sites, including volcanoes, earthquakes, and tsunamis: **gcmd.gsfc.nasa.gov/Resources/pointers/hazards.html**
- For amazing volcanic images and tips on how to build a volcano model: **http://volcano.und.nodak.edu**

Glossary

AA A Hawaiian word used to describe thick, lumpy lava that forms angular lumps when cool.

AFTERSHOCKS Smaller earth tremors that happen after an earthquake. These may occur for several days or even weeks after the main tremor.

ASH AND DUST In volcanology, these terms refer to the smallest fragments of lava formed when a volcano explodes. Small pieces are called ash, and the powder-fine particles are known as dust.

BASALT The most common volcanic rock. Basalt is formed by runny lavas and is dark and fine-grained.

BLACK SMOKER A volcanic hot spring on the ocean floor that spits out black water containing metal sulfides and oxides.

BOMBS AND BLOCKS Large pieces of lava that are thrown out during a volcanic eruption. Bombs are slightly rounded in shape, while blocks are more angular.

CALDERA A giant crater or bowl-shaped depression at the top of a volcano, formed when the summit collapses into the volcano's magma chamber. Calderas can be many miles across.

CARBONIZE To turn to carbon. Objects that contain carbon will turn to carbon (or charcoal), rather than burn, when there is not enough oxygen available for them to burn in the usual way.

Carbonized walnuts from Pompeii

The crater of Mount Vesuvius, Italy

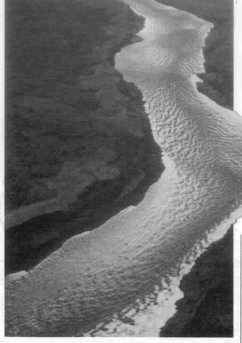

A red-hot flow of aa lava, Hawaii

CONTINENTAL DRIFT Continent movement caused by plate tectonics.

CORE The center of Earth, made up of dense metals, in particular iron. The inner core is solid while the outer core is liquid metal.

CRATER Hollow depression formed when the cone of a volcano collapses inward. Also known as a caldera.

CRATER LAKE Lake formed when water fills the crater or caldera of a volcano.

DORMANT The term used to describe a volcano that has not been active for more than several hundred years but was active within the last several thousand years.

EPICENTER The point on Earth's surface, directly above the focus, or point of origin, of an earthquake.

EXTINCT The term used to describe a volcano that has not been active for over several thousand years.

FAULT A fracture in rock along which blocks of rock slide past each other.

FEEDER PIPE The long tube magma passes through from the magma chamber to the surface.

FISSURE A crack in the ground. A fissure eruption is one where runny lava flows from a crack in the ground.

FOCUS The point within Earth's mantle from which an earthquake originates.

A geyser in Iceland

FUMAROLE A vent or opening in Earth's surface that emits steam or gas.

GEOLOGY The study of the history and development of Earth's rocks and past life.

GEYSER A place where water that has been superheated by hot magma underground bursts up into the air.

HOT SPOT A place in the middle of a tectonic plate, rather than at the boundary, where columns of magma from the mantle rise up through the crust, creating a volcano.

HYDROTHERMAL VENT A place where mineral-rich water heated by hot magma underground erupts onto the surface. Geysers, black smokers, and hot springs are all hydrothermal vents.

IGNEOUS ROCKS Rocks formed as hot magma and lava cools.

INTENSITY The term used to describe the severity of the shaking experienced during an earthquake. It is usually measured using the modified Mercalli intensity scale.

LAHAR A mudflow made up of large quantities of volcanic fragments and water. Also known as a mudflow.

LAPILLI Small fragments of lava, formed as the magma bursts out of a volcano.

LAVA Hot, molten rock that is emitted from a volcano.

LAVA TUBE A tunnel of lava created when the surface of a lava flow cools and hardens to form a roof, while hot, molten lava continues to flow inside it.

MAGMA Hot, molten rock originating from within Earth.

MAGMA CHAMBER Area beneath a volcano where magma builds up before an eruption.

MAGNITUDE The term used to describe the severity or scale of an earthquake. This is calculated or measured in several different ways, the most common of which is the Richter scale.

MANTLE The layer inside the Earth between the crust and the core. The mantle is 1,800 miles (2,900 km) thick.

MERCALLI SCALE The scale for measuring the intensity of an earthquake by observing its effects.

MID-OCEAN RIDGE A mountain ridge on the ocean floor formed where two tectonic plates meet.

MUDFLOW A fast-moving stream of mud, water, and often volcanic ash and pumice. Also known as a lahar.

NUÉE ARDENTE French for "glowing cloud." The term used to describe the strange clouds of a pyroclastic flow when they are a mix of cloud and hot ash.

PAHOEHOE The Hawaiian term for hot, runny lava that flows quickly and, usually, in quite shallow flows.

PILLOW LAVA Rounded lava formations shaped when lava erupts gently underwater.

PLATE TECTONICS The theory that Earth's surface is broken up into large slabs or plates. The seven large plates and various smaller plates are constantly moving at the rate of a few inches per year. Most volcanoes and earthquakes are found at the boundaries of these plates.

RING OF FIRE The area encircling the Pacific Ocean where most volcanic and earthquake activity occurs.

Pumice

SEISMIC WAVES The vibrations, or shock waves, that radiate out from the focus of an earthquake.

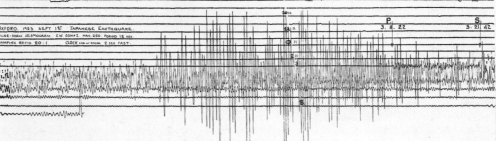
Seismogram of the 1923 Tokyo earthquake

Aa lava

Pahoehoe lava

PLUG An obstruction of solidified magma in the neck of a volcano.

PUMICE Lightweight volcanic rock filled with holes formed by the bubbles of gas in the lava.

PYROCLASTIC FLOW A burning cloud of gas, dust, ash, rocks, and bombs that flows down the mountain after an explosive eruption. If the cloud is made up of more gas than ash, it is known as a pyroclastic surge.

P WAVES The fastest and first or "primary" waves of an earthquake.

RICHTER SCALE Scale for measuring the total energy released by earthquakes and recorded seismographs. The scale ranges from 1 to 10, with 10 the most severe end of the scale. Each whole number increase corresponds to an increase of about 32 times the amount of energy released.

SEISMOMETER A machine for detecting earthquake shock waves is called a seismometer. A machine that records the information is called a seismograph.

SEISMOGRAM The record produced by a seismograph showing the pattern of shock waves from an earthquake.

SUBDUCTION ZONE Where two tectonic plates meet and one plate is pushed down into the mantle, partially melting rocks. The resulting magma erupts at the surface through volcanoes.

S WAVES The slower, "secondary" waves of an earthquake.

TSUNAMI Fast-moving waves caused by earthquakes or volcanic eruption displacing the ocean floor and water.

VENT The opening through which a volcanic eruption occurs.

VOLCANOLOGIST A scientist who studies volcanoes.

Volcanologists collecting gas samples on Colima volcano, in Mexico

Index

Acknowledgments

Dorling Kindersley would like to thank:
John Lepine & Jane Insley of the Science Museum, London; Robert Symes, Colin Keates & Tim Parmenter of the Natural History Museum, London; the staff at the Museo Archeologico di Napoli; Giuseppe Luongo, Luigi Iadicicco, & Vincenzo D'Errico at the Vesuvius Observatory for help in photographing the instruments on pp. 49, 53 & 55; Paul Arthur; Paul Cole; Lina Ferrante at Pompeii; Dott. Angarano at Solfatara; Carlo Illario at Herculaneum; Roger Musson of the British Geological Survey; Joe Cann; Tina Chambers for extra photography; Gin von Noorden & Helena Spiteri for editorial assistance; Céline Carez for research & development; Wilfred Wood & Earl Neish for design assistance; Jane Parker for the index; Stewart J. Wild for proof-reading; David Ekholm–JAlbum, Sunita Gahir, Susan St. Louis, Carey Scott, Lisa Stock, & Bulent Yusuf for the clip art; Neville Graham, Sue Nicholson, & Susan St. Louis for the wall chart; and Christine Heilman for Americanization.

Illustrations: John Woodcock.

Maps: Sallie Alane Reason.

Models: David Donkin (pp. 8–9, 50–51)&Edward Laurence Associates (pp. 12-13).

Picture credits:
a-above; b-below; c-center; l-left; r-right; t-top

Ancient Art & Architecture Collection: 47t. Art Directors Photo Library: 47tc, 49tc. B.F.I.: 46cr, 57cr. Bridgeman Art Library: 6tl & c. Musee des Beaux-Arts, Lille: 44tl. British Museum: 27tr & c. Herge/Casterman: 20tl. Dr Joe Cann, University of Leeds: 25bc. Jean-Loup Charmet: 27bl, 31tl, 46bl, 51tl. Circus World Museum, Baraboo, Wisconsin: 32br. Corbis: Bettmann 67tl; Danny Lehman 65cr;Vittoriano Rastelli 70tc; Roger Ressmeyer 71br; Jim Sugar Photography 67b. Eric Crichton 41tr, 41bl. Culver Pictures Inc: 60br. DK Images: Satellite Imagemap © 1996–2003 Planetary Visions 9c. Earthquake Research Institute, University of Tokyo: 63cr. Edimedia/Russian Museum, Leningrad: 28cl. E.T. Archive: 49c, 58tr, 62tl. Mary Evans Picture Library: 8tc, 16tl, 26tl, 27br, 28c, 29cr, 46tl, 64cr, 66br. Le Figaro Magazine/Philippe Bourseiller: 19t, 19cl 19bl, 19br, 35tr. Fiorepress: 49br. Gallimard: 44tr. Getty Images: 59bl. G.S.F.: 13tl, 14bl; /Frank Fitch: 20c. John Guest c.NASA: 44bl. Robert Harding Picture Library: 12tl, 14tr, 15cr 17tr, 17cr, 20tr, 21br, 63br, 24tl, 38br, 39br, 40tr, 42c, 43br, 48br, 49bl, 51tr, 60lc, 62bl, 62-63c, Explorer 66bl. Bruce C. Heezen & Marie Tharp, 1977/c.

Marie Tharp: 11c. Historical Pictures Service, Inc.: 10cr. Michael Holford: 22tr. Illustrated London News: 60bl. ImageState: 68bc. Katz Pictures: Alberto Garcia/Saba 64b. Frank Lane Picture Agency: 23rct, 23c. Frank Lane Picture Agency/S.Jonasson: 41tc, 49cr. Archive Larousse-Giraudon: 32cl. London Fire Brigade/LFCDA: 58bl. Mansell Collection: 31tr. NASA: 24bc, 55cr, 68-69. Natural History Museum: 34tl. National Maritime Museum: 8tl. Orion Press: 7tr, 61bl. Oxford Scientific Films/Colin Monteath: 69br; / NASA: 69cl; /Kim Westerkov: 11bl; 15tl. PA Photos: Andy Eames/AP 57cl. Planet Earth Pictures/Franz J.Camenzind: 7cr; /D.Weisel: 17br; / James D. Watt: 23rcb; /Robert Hessler: 25tr, 25lc. Popperfoto: 6b, 11tr, 54bl. R.C.S. Rizzoli: 48lc. Rex Features: 67tr. Gary Rosenquist: 14tl, 14br, 15tr, 15br. Scala: 7c, 49bl(inset); /Louvre: 63tr. Science Photo Library/Earth Sattelite Corp.: 7tl; /Peter Menzel: 7br, 20br, 46cl, 65bl; /David Parker: 13tr, 61tl, 61tr, 65tc; /Ray Fairbanks: 18c; /Inst Oceanographic Sciences: 24c; /Matthew Shipp: 24bl; /NASA: 35c, 43cr, 44cr, 44c, 44-45b; /U.S.G.S.: 45tr; /Peter Ryan: 55tr; /David Weintraub 66t. Frank Spooner Pictures: 8cl, 16cr, 17tl, 22bl, 23tr, 23br, 35tc, 42cl, 47cl, 49cl, 56tl, 56bl, 57bl, 58tl, 59tr, 59br, 61clcb; /Nigel Hicks 69tr. Syndication International: 31cr; /Inst. Geological Science: 32tc, 35br, 41tl, 47br; /Daily Mirror: 54tr, 57tr. Susanna van Rose: 39bl. Woods Hole Oceanographic Institute/Rod Catanach: 24br; /Dudley Foster: 25bl; /J.Frederick Grassle: 25tc; /Robert Hessler: 25tl.

ZEFA: 9tl, 21tl, 34bl, 45br, 57br.

Wall chart credits: Corbis: Burstein Collection / Barney Burstein fbr; Roger Ressmeyer cra; DK Images: Museo Archeologico Nazionale di Napoli cr; Natural History Museum, London clb (aa lava), cra (pyroclastic debris); Getty Images: Image Bank / G. Brad Lewis cla (Pahoehoe flow); National Geographic / Klaus Nigge ca; NASA: crb; Science Photo Library: Peter Menzel br (San Francisco)

Jacket credits: Front: Alamy Images: Douglas Peebles Photography c; Corbis: Bettman cra; DK Images: Natural History Museum, London tl (agate-lined geode); Science Photo Library: NASA tr. Back: The Bridgeman Art Library: br; DK Images: Museo Archeologico Nazionale di Napoli tl; Natural History Museum, London cla, cra, l.

All other images © Dorling Kindersley. For further information, see: www.dkimages.com